Getting

Stoned

with

Savages

ALSO BY J. MAARTEN TROOST

The Sex Lives of Cannibals

Broadway Books   New York

Getting Stoned with Savages

A TRIP THROUGH THE ISLANDS OF FIJI AND VANUATU

J. Maarten Troost

PUBLISHED BY BROADWAY BOOKS

Published in the United States by Broadway Books,
an imprint of The Doubleday Broadway Publishing Group,
a division of Random House, Inc., New York.
www.broadwaybooks.com

BROADWAY BOOKS and its logo, a letter B bisected on the diagonal,
are trademarks of Random House, Inc.

Book design by Elizabeth Rendfleisch
Illustrations by Andrew Barthelmes

Library of Congress Cataloging-in-Publication Data

Troost, J. Maarten.
    Getting stoned with savages : a trip through the islands of Fiji and Vanuatu /
J. Maarten Troost.—1st ed.
        p. c.m.
    1. Fiji—Description and travel. 2. Vanuatu—Description and travel. 3. Troost,
J. Maarten—Travel—Fiji. 4. Troost, J. Maarten—Travel—Vanuatu. 5. Fiji—Social
life and customs. 6. Vanuatu—Social life and customs. I. Title.

DU600.T75 2006
919.59504—dc22   2006042612

ISBN-13: 978-0-7679-2199-2
ISBN-10: 0-7679-2199-2

PRINTED IN THE UNITED STATES OF AMERICA

10 9 8 7 6 5 4 3

DISCLAIMER

The author acknowledges that he is not Bob Woodward. Mr. Woodward is scrupulous with names and dates. This author is not. Mr. Woodward would never suggest that something happened in October when, in fact, it occurred in April. This author would. Mr. Woodward recounts conversations as they actually occurred. This author would like to do that, but alas, he does not excel at penmanship and he cannot read his notes. However, the author has an excellent memory. You can trust him.

For Sylvia, Lukas, and Samuel

 CONTENTS

Chapter 4   54

IN WHICH the author is introduced to kava, which he likes very much, oh yes, very much indeed.

Chapter 5   75

IN WHICH the author is reduced to a state of wondrous awe as the prime minister of Vanuatu conspires to sell his country in exchange for a ruby, a giant ruby, which curiously no one is allowed to examine.

Chapter 6   83

IN WHICH the author ponders cannibalism and discovers that he just doesn't get it—not at all, cannot get past the icky factor—and so, left to his own devices by his beguiling wife, he decides to seek enlightenment on the island of Malekula, where until recently, within his own lifetime even, they lunched on people.

Chapter 7   117

IN WHICH the author experiences his first cyclone, causing him to reconsider his position on Nature—whether he's for it or against it—and after a terrifying encounter with a giant centipede seems to have settled the issue, his wife gives him News, which only complicates the matter further.

Chapter 8   134

IN WHICH the author travels to the island of Tanna, where he ascends an active volcano; witnesses the extraordinary Nekowiar ceremony, culminating with the slaughter of two hundred pigs; and meets with villagers deep within the forest who live according to the tenets of *kastom*, which is another word for naked.

Getting
Stoned
with
Savages

In which the author, much to his surprise, finds himself holding down a job, a real job that could possibly lead to a career, which causes him considerable distress as he envisions his world reduced to swirling acronyms, whereupon his beguiling wife offers him another way, an escape, an alternate road, and together they decide to move to the distant islands of the South Pacific.

I HAVE BEEN CALLED MANY THINGS IN MY LIFE, BUT IF there has been but one constant, one barb, one arrow flung my way time after time, it is the accusation that I am, in essence, nothing more than an escapist. Apparently this is bad, suspect, possibly even un-American. Mention to someone that, all things being equal, you'd really rather be on an island in the South Pacific, and they'll look at you quizzically, ponder the madness of the notion for a moment, and say: "But that's just escapism. Now would you kindly finish stocking the paper clips so we have time to rearrange the Hi-Liter markers? We need to make sure they're color-coordinated."

I'm not sure where this tendency came from. Escapism, we are led to believe, is evidence of a deficiency in character, a certain failure of temperament, and like so many -isms, it is to be strenuously avoided. How do you expect to get ahead? people ask. But the question altogether misses the point. The escapist doesn't want to get ahead. He simply wants to get away. I understand this, for I am an unapologetic escapist. Once before, I had abandoned the life I knew in Washington, D.C., escaping the urgent din of the continental world for a distant atoll in the equatorial Pacific. I lived there for two years, never once looking at a clock, marveling at what a strange turn my life had taken. *I may have heat rash,* I thought back then, *and I might be hosting eight different kinds of parasites, but at least I'm not some office drone.* I had escaped, I thought mirthfully as I tended to my septic infections. And then, suddenly, my life took another dramatic U-turn, and I once again found myself back in Washington, where every morning I was confronted by a debilitating decision: What tie to wear?

The dissonance was overwhelming. One day, I found myself pressed inside the Washington Metro, soaked through from a November rain, palpitating slightly as I realized I had an 8 A.M. meeting and it was presently 8:17 A.M., and just like that it occurred to me that six months earlier I could be found paddling an outrigger canoe across the sun-dappled waters of a lagoon in the South Pacific. This had been happening for some time, this juxtaposition of my former life upon my present one, and the contrast never failed to leave me twitching in bafflement. *How had this happened?* Huddled on the subway, I lingered on the image for a moment, far away, envisioning the canopy of palm trees swaying in the near distance, the urgent leap of a flying fish, the fishermen in sailing canoes returning with their catch, the brilliant, shimmering colors offered by a setting sun, until my reverie came to an abrupt end as the subway doors opened and I was swept into the tumult of the rush-hour commute. It was a disconcerting sensation. *Blue, blue water,* I thought in vain as I was shepherded onto an escalator crowded with pasty-faced suits like myself, dejected already. I tried imagining *swaying palm trees* as I scurried through the rain toward my office at the World Bank, flashing the color-coded ID card I kept tethered to my belt. Inside, I tried conjuring *stress-free tropical living* once I found on my chair a dreaded note from my boss: PLEASE SEE ME. 7:45 A.M. But the image was gone. *Poof.*

How had this happened? I wondered again. For two years I had lived in Kiribati, a widely dispersed scattering of atolls at the end of the world, where I had led a rather lively and adventurous existence with my girlfriend Sylvia. And now I was right back where I started, in the real world, as some prefer to call it, wondering how I might leave it again.

As I settled into my office, I noticed another note on top of my keyboard, scrawled by the office assistant: IFC MEETING IN WBIGF CONFERENCE ROOM. WHERE ARE YOU??? 8:21 A.M. The message light on my phone blinked ominously. Sighing, I loped toward the conference room, pausing briefly to catch sight of my reflection in the window, and I noted with some interest that I looked like sodden vermin. It was not going to be a good day, I knew. The conference room itself was transparent, because the World Bank values transparency, and as I approached I wondered, *Is that a Bank vice president sitting there? Why, yes, it was. Is that another one?* Indeed so. *And look, there's our division chief. Does he ever look pissed off.* I entered, and as I mumbled my apologies, my boss cut me off. "Finally," he said. "Now we can begin. Do you have the PowerPoint slides?"

"Er . . . the PowerPoint slides . . . was that me? . . . I thought . . . Wasn't Sergio . . . ?"

Sergio looked upon me with serene blankness. I dampened a little further as the perspiration commingled with the rain, and as I studied the multitude of agitated faces, I thought to myself, *Six months ago . . .*

Inexplicably, six months turned into a year, and then two. Yet, that strange sense of dislocation never left me. *Where am I?* I'd ask myself with alarming frequency. *How did I get here? What events in time and space have brought me to this moment?* Glancing out my office window, I'd see limousines depositing presidents and prime ministers, Nobel laureates and eminent thinkers, even Bono himself, and I'd remember that not so long ago I had lived in a place that could not possibly be further removed from the global stage. In Kiribati, I would gladly have given up a finger or two for a newspaper, and now here I was, surrounded by newsworthy personalities. Even my friends thought my change in circumstances odd.

"The World Bank? You? You're a hoity-toity consultant to the World Bank?" asked one.

"Yes."

"You were unemployed for two years, and now you've got this glam job at the World Bank?"

"I wasn't unemployed," I countered, pleased to hear someone describe my job as glamorous.

"I see. And what was it you did for two years?"

"I was writing."

"Writing." Long pause here. "And how much, if you don't mind my asking, did your writing—and I'm sure it was sublime—how much money, would you say, did your writing earn you?"

"Net?"

"Yes, net.

"Three hundred and fifty dollars."

"*Three hundred and fifty dollars.*" This was savored for a moment. "Two years. Three hundred and fifty dollars."

"Three hundred and fifty American dollars."

"Three hundred and fifty *American* dollars, then. And now you advise countries, entire countries, on what they should do with their money."

"Actually, my boss does that."

"And so what do you do?"

"I help him."

"You help him. And for this help, you are no doubt handsomely remunerated."

"I can't complain."

I couldn't, really. For the first time in my life I had more money than I knew what to do with. This, like so much else, was a startling change in circumstances. For years I had lived the easy poverty of the vagabond. And just as everyone else was boarding the Internet money train, I disappeared to the far side of the world, where I lived as a financial parasite while hacking away at a novel that meandered into failure. Money—the possession thereof—should have made me giddy with joy. And it did. For a day. The day I saw my bank account surge into the four figures, which seemed a stratospheric sum. But then, what to do with it? I mean, after the restaurant splurges. And your need for Paris has been sated. Where do you put it? In stocks? Bonds? That's what I did. And here's the funny thing. Then you begin to worry about money. To my everlasting disappointment, I discovered that it's true what they say. Money doesn't buy you happiness.

Damn it.

It was all so very baffling to me. I had money. I had a respectable job. If I tried just a little bit harder and played my cards right, I could turn my consultancy into a permanent staff position and then I would be set for life. I could move on from WBILG to WBOPA, maybe even to WBPCL. And from there all sorts of possibilities opened up: UNDP, EBRD, IMF, ADB, maybe even a job with the bad boys over at IFC. Well, perhaps not the IFC. That meeting had not gone very well. Not at all. I had made my boss look bad, a big no-no at the World Bank. But still, if I simply applied myself, I could count on lifetime employment as a well-compensated international bureaucrat with all the perks the job entailed. There would be business-class travel and six weeks of annual vacation. There would be health insurance and an extremely generous pension. And best of all, I could never, ever be fired. Once encased within the United Nations system, a staffer is guaranteed lifetime employment, perhaps not as a rule, but most certainly in practice. The office next to mine, for instance, was occupied by a Korean gentleman who, as far as anyone could tell, had not produced even a suggestion of work in well over three years. Some days he showed up, some days not, and yet every year his salary percolated ever upward. It wasn't quite what I aspired to, but I did recognize that there are much, much worse ways to make a living.

Yet, I didn't apply myself any harder. Instead, as I stared forlornly at my computer screen, trying halfheartedly to decipher a complex economic equation ("No math," I had told them. "I'm one hundred percent right brain"), I found that very soon, once again, my thoughts drifted toward the Pacific. Two years ago, I remembered, I was on an outer island in Kiribati, resting in a thatch-roofed meeting house and chatting amiably with an elderly man about the dozens of shark fins drying in the rafters. I didn't think much of it at the time. It was just a normal day in Kiribati. But now, as I perused my wall, the stacks of heavy binders with titles like *Privatization and the Energy Sector* and *Infrastructure Finance: A Global Challenge,* binders piled so high that they nearly covered the ubiquitous Monet print—how I hated those lilies—I found that I nearly ached at the recollection. Once, my world had been filled with wonder and mystery. I lived surrounded by water so blue that I sometimes gasped at the beauty of it. I knew magicians and sorcerers. I slept under multitudes of stars and finally understood what is meant by the spiritual world. I . . .

"You're forgetting the human feces on the beach," said my wife,

Sylvia, a little later, just as my exposition was beginning to roll. Sylvia was the girlfriend I had followed to Kiribati. We had faked marriage there, and after two years of practice we felt we had earned the rings. "You're also forgetting ringworm, dengue fever, and 'La Macarena.' And do you remember when the beer was sent to the wrong island? You weren't waxing poetic then. And the food— months of nothing but rice and rotten fish. Do you remember that Christmas package your dad sent, the one with all the cookies and chocolate?"

Indeed I did. It was a Christmas tradition begun by my grandmother in Holland. Every year, she sent us packages containing the buttery sweets and milky chocolates that the Dutch excel in producing. My father had taken up the tradition after my grandmother passed away. The package he sent had taken seven months to reach us in Kiribati, and by the time it arrived more than half its contents had been consumed by rats, with the remainder scarred by claws and fangs. It never occurred to us not to eat it. We devoured the remaining half in one long gluttonous afternoon, feeling nothing but blissful rapture.

"But wasn't that the best chocolate you ever had?" I asked.

"Yes," she sighed. "But that's the point. I never want to feel that desperate again."

She did have a point. Escapism is not without its costs. Life had been desperate in Kiribati. Whatever hopes we'd had of finding the South Seas idyll of our imagination were cruelly dashed by the realities of island living. True, it had been beautiful. But it had also been hard. Living in a state of perpetual denial, as we did in Kiribati, had a way of heightening one's appreciation of the small things, like chocolate. But strangely, I didn't appreciate chocolate anymore. Indeed, I couldn't remember the last time I'd even *had* chocolate, and for some reason, this had begun to bother me, for what is life, a good life, but the accumulation of small pleasures? In Washington, we lived in a place where everything was available, for a price, and yet I couldn't recall the last time I had really savored something—a book, a sunset, a fine meal. It was as if the sensory overload that is American life had somehow led to sensory deprivation, a gilded weariness, where everything is permitted and nothing appreciated. I'd find myself inside a Whole Foods, and remember that not long ago I would have engaged in all sorts of criminality for a chance to skip down these heaving aisles, yet now I found myself feeling a mite peeved that the cheese selection wasn't quite as expansive as I would have wished. In Kiribati I yearned for all that we had in Washington—high-end grocery stores, reliable electricity, endless consumer choice—and now that I was in the midst of all this bounty, I pined for what we had in Kiribati, the intangibles at least, for there are no tangibles to be found on a remote atoll.

Mostly, however, and this was what I kept tripping over as I put on my tie each morning, I recalled that life in Kiribati had been ceaselessly interesting. True, not always in a good way. Indeed, now that Sylvia had stirred my memories, I remembered that life in the South Pacific could be grim, often horrifying, and frequently revolting. One morning, I recalled, I had awoken to find a dead pig in our backyard. This was no small problem on the equator. There is nothing like the odor of dead swine decomposing under the tropical sun to help one decide what the day's priorities are going to be. It took the better part of the morning to dispose of the bloated beast. I found a large stick and I pushed and prodded the pig toward the incoming tide. *Please, ocean,* I said, *just take the pig.* But it wouldn't. The pig floated, and each time I pushed it out into the water the ocean pushed it right back at me, depositing the carcass with a grotesque thud at my feet. This greatly amused the I-Kiribati onlookers, until finally one man took pity. We each took a hoof in hand and pulled the rotting pig about three hundred yards through the surf toward reef's edge, where with a mighty heave we tossed it into the white water. "A present for the sharks," my companion had said. That's when I noticed that my hands, my arms, and much of my torso were stained with dead-pig slime. I don't think I have ever swum faster.

Now why, one may reasonably ask, would anyone want to go back to such a world? This is an excellent question. Boredom, a ferocious, unyielding boredom certainly played a part. That morning in Kiribati, I had managed, in a few short hours, to do something productive. I had disposed of a problem. I had swum in the Pacific Ocean. I had sensed danger. I had made a friend. I had a new story to tell. Certainly, I would not want to relive that particular day, but at least something had happened. Something interesting. While it may be true that finding a decomposing pig in your yard is not an ideal way to begin one's day, I found that beginning each new day in Washington, as I did, with the shocking blast of an alarm clock buzzer, shortly to be followed by a frantic race to the office, where I would be greeted by a computer with the news that I had ninety-two new messages, of which thirty-seven were alleged to be urgent, and then to spend the remainder of the day stressing mightily about agendas and bullet points, memos and PowerPoint presentations, conferences and conference calls, only to call it quits long after sunset with the queasy realization that after all that time, all that energy, all that fussing, I really had nothing to show for my day, nothing real and tangible and good—well, I found that such a day stinks too.

In Washington, we were led to believe that we inhabited the center of the world, that the rest of the globe spun according to our whims and priorities. This can be a heady feeling. Should the Namibians have electricity? We decide. Should the Laotians be able to trade sugarcane? If they would just ask nicely. Is the Haitian gov-

ernment getting uppity? Fuck 'em. We're taking them out. This tends
to attract a certain kind of person, and when I looked at myself in the
mirror and noticed my gray suit, my Brooks Brothers shirt, my silk
tie, and my soft leather Italian shoes, I realized that I was not such a
person. I felt like a tourist, dreamily walking through a life that was
not meant to be mine. Some people are attracted to power. I'd rather
be plucking at a ukulele on a faraway beach. I was not a soft-leather-
Italian-shoe kind of man. I was a flip-flop man. And as a flip-flop
man I knew what needed to be done. Kiribati may not have been paradise, but I was ready to keep looking. I knew how to do it too. My
wife would have to find another job in the South Pacific.

IT WAS SO EASY, REALLY. Unexpectedly so.

"The South Pacific would do nothing for my career," Sylvia had
countered.

"Career, schmeer." *Blue, blue water.*

"And it would mean a pay cut."

"I have money, and if it runs out, well, we can live off love."
Swaying palm trees.

"But I do think the South Pacific would be a great place to start
a family."

"Er . . ."

My wife, clearly, was an out-of-the-box thinker. It had been my
understanding that when women felt the urge to procreate, it was
usually accompanied by a need to settle down, to own a house, perhaps even in the suburbs, where the schools are rumored to be good
and the neighbors chirpy. Not Sylvia. The motherhood instinct had
somehow elicited a desire to flee, to remove herself as far as possible
from America. She too had experienced the bewildering dissonance,

the extreme culture shock that was the inevitable result of moving from a place like Kiribati to a city like Washington. Perhaps she wasn't as inclined to romanticizing island life as I was, but there was enough of the islander in her for her to conclude that, all things being equal, she'd rather have children on an island far, far away. "It takes a village," she said. "There are no villages left in America." What fortuitous timing, I thought. I also had the urge to flee. And if it meant that sex might lead to a little bundle of consequences, well, I thought, abstractly, that would be pretty wonderful too.

Soon there was a job for Sylvia. The organization that she had worked for in Kiribati, the Foundation for the Peoples of the South Pacific, had asked her to be the regional manager, a position that was based in Fiji. Fiji, of course, was not Kiribati. We knew this from experience. After we left Kiribati, we had spent a month traveling around the South Pacific, including to Fiji. Knowing its status as a favored destination for the rich and the beautiful, we were fairly confident that we were unlikely to encounter the deprivation that had so defined our experience in Kiribati. If Fiji was good enough for Nicole Kidman, we reasoned, it was good enough for us. Suddenly, life was looking pretty good. We had a plan. A fine plan, I thought. We would move to Fiji, the happy islands. I would write a book about Kiribati, and if that didn't work out, there was always yam farming. Sylvia would do noble and uplifting work for the good people of the South Pacific. Our house would echo with the pitter-patter of little feet. With the future looking so bright, I felt confident enough to start hitting the snooze button.

And then our plan went up in smoke. I arrived at work one morning, comfortably after 9 A.M., more like 10 A.M., well rested, refreshed, and as I scrolled through my e-mail, there in the midst of innumerable agendas and consultant reports was a message with the heading COUP! That caught my eye. It was a mass mailing sent by an acquaintance of ours in Fiji. *We're safe now*, it began, which I thought was a very lively way to begin an e-mail. The message was a stream-of-consciousness recounting of a very bad day. *Gunmen . . . prime minister held hostage . . . shooting . . . looters . . . Suva on fire.*

Sylvia called. "Did you hear?"

"Yes. But hopefully this will resolve itself soon."

But it didn't resolve itself. On that balmy morning in Fiji, a group of men armed with automatic guns and machetes had entered the parliament in Suva, the capital, and taken the prime minister and much of the government hostage. Typically, the South Pacific receives nary a mention in the world press, with the notable exception of the occasional celebrity sighting in Tahiti. Now, however, the back pages of newspapers around the world were full of stories with headlines like TOURISTS TERRORIZED AT POSH ISLAND RESORT. There had been a previous coup in Fiji, in 1987, and the wits in the press began to refer to Fiji as "coup-coup land." We consumed all the news we could find, hoping that the coup would prove to be a mere blip, a temporary usurpation of law and order, and that the tensions would quietly dissolve with a kava ceremony, an apology, a group hug, and the solemn exchange of a whale's tooth. But as the hostage drama unfolded over the following fifty-six days, and as we watched aghast as the television broadcast images of Suva in flames, it grew harder to maintain the illusion that this was anything other than a very serious problem. Nevertheless, I kept trying. We had a plan. Coup or no coup. Until one day, Sylvia came home and declared: "Fiji has been postponed."

"Alas," I said. "I had rather been counting on moving to Fiji."

"So was I. But, you know, there's been a coup."

"Which would make living in Fiji even more interesting," I contended. "It's not the first coup there. The other one turned out fine."

"But this time they're killing each other."

"Yes, it's terrible. It's just that . . . well, I got fired today."

"You were fired?"

"Well, they were very nice about it, saying that they were declining to renew my contract, funding issues and the like, and that they would think of me in the future, but their meaning was quite clear. I cleaned out my desk. So, you see, I was thinking that moving to the South Pacific now would work out pretty well as my schedule is, well, presently rather open."

"I can't believe you got fired." Sylvia shook her head.

"It's not my proudest moment."

"Well, fortunately for you, they'd like to base the job in Vanuatu for the time being. Still willing to go?"

Out of the ashes, a new plan.

CHAPTER 2

In which the author offers some interesting arcana about Vanuatu—its one-hundred-some languages, its history of cannibalism, its cargo cults, its smoldering volcanoes—and arrives on the island of Efate, where he soon gets stuck.

AND SO VANUATU. THIS REALLY WAS A MOST FORTU-nate turn of events, and it made the sting of being an unemployed consultant cast out of the halls of power exceedingly bearable. While I would have preferred to have delivered a decisive *I quit*, the important thing was that the deed was done, and as I wandered the streets of Washington with a sprightly spring in my flip-flops I was beginning to feel more than a little smug. *Yeah, you there,* I thought, spying a harried-looking lawyer clutching an Au Bon Pain sandwich with one hand while the other was weighed down by a forty-pound briefcase. *An associate, aren't you, working ninety hours a week, no life to speak of . . . ? I'm off to the South Pacific.* Seeing a young woman staggering with two laptops as she struggled to keep up with a very important looking fellow carrying the lightest of cell phones, I thought, *Intern! You poor thing. Get out now . . . Melanesia, baby, Melanesia.*

It was all so very liberating, because not only were we returning to the South Pacific with all its attendant beauty and languor; we were going to Vanuatu. I had once before alighted upon the islands of Vanuatu, and while I had been there for only one short week, I re-called feeling that the country was very likely one of the oddest on Earth. Mind you, I had just spent two years on an atoll, utterly iso-lated from the greater world, and so I was in a frame of mind to be addled. But there was something peculiar about Vanuatu, an endur-ing strangeness that I found particularly appealing. As I tossed my suits and ties into a bag bound for charity, I couldn't have been hap-pier. Begone, gray suits. I won't be needing you anymore. I'm off to an island nation where formal wear consists of a leaf tied around a penis.

As we packed, I recalled all the mistakes I had made preparing for island life in Kiribati. Packing for the South Pacific is different from packing for other regions. This was more like packing by sub-traction. Sweaters, pants, socks—gone, gone, gone. Couch? Table and chairs? In the Pacific, one sits on the floor. As the days passed we divested ourselves of much of our clothing, all of our furniture, and soon little remained of our lives except a couple of suitcases heavy with tattered shorts and floral-print shirts. I am very fond of new beginnings. Indeed, I daresay I rather excel at new beginnings. One invariably becomes good at something when one does it often enough. It pleased me that after thirty-some years of life, the bag-gage I carried could be reduced to one suitcase.

With the day of our departure nearing, our minds turned to Vanuatu. The impression we had taken from our short stay there two years earlier was that these islands constituted one unusual lit-tle nation. The geography itself accounts for no small measure of the country's strangeness. This is because Vanuatu's eighty-some is-lands lie directly on the Pacific Ring of Fire, which, as the name im-plies, is a rather fearsome place to find oneself. There is quite likely no greater force than that created when one tectonic plate with, let's say, Australia and the Indian subcontinent on its back decides to get personal with another tectonic plate carrying, oh, how about the mass of the Pacific Ocean, the west coasts of North and South America, and, for good measure, Japan on its shoulders. Yet this is where Vanuatu finds itself, and what an exciting place it is, geologically speaking. "As solid as the earth below one's feet" is not an expression often used in Vanuatu. The islands are young, temperamental adolescents, prone to mood swings and sudden growth spurts, and it is not uncommon for an island in Vanuatu to experience a sudden jolt and find itself thrust upward another yard or two. Now and then, an island loses it altogether and, in an apoplectic fit, blows itself up entirely, as happened to Kuwae in 1452. And always there are the earthquakes—many, many, earthquakes—that happen each and every day. Most are inconsequential, mere tremors. Though for those, like me, who have never before seen cutlery dance across a table in a restaurant, they can still be vividly disturbing.

"What was that?" I had asked the waitress in Port Vila, the capital, once I had reclaimed my wits.

"That was calamari."

"No, no. That shaking, what was that?"

"Nothing. Just a little earthquake, a hiccup."

A hiccup, most likely, caused by the belching of one of Vanuatu's nine active volcanoes. True, two of them are underwater, but seven living volcanoes occupying a land mass not much greater than Connecticut is an astonishing concentration of raw, Vulcan power. In Vanuatu, the Earth is alive and well, thank you, and it is there where one can experience the awesome might of the planet. To stand upon the rim of such a volcano, even when it is merely wheezing, sending forth with surly indifference the occasional car-sized boulder or a long, snotty stream of flaming magma, is to behold the immense potency of Earth. *Do not trifle with me,* you sense it telling you, and immediately you want to throw a few Hummer owners over the rim, a small offering to the gods. Alas, it's not the owners of monster

SUVs who suffer when the planet is feeling particularly churlish—not yet, in any case. The people of Ambrym, an island with the distinction of having two exceedingly energetic volcanoes on its shores, have suffered through forty-eight major eruptions since 1774. If the people of Ambrym seem a little skittish to the outsider, a little prone to pessimism and ill humor, there is a very good reason for it. It affects one's sensibilities, the knowledge that at any moment your world can go *boom.*

One would think that in a place where the land itself is frequently prone to vigorous shaking and intemperate explosions, nature would, at the very least, grant a pleasant climate. One would be wrong. While Vanuatu has wonderfully fair weather for half the year, the other half is occupied by cyclones. From November through April, the islands can reliably expect to be walloped by two or three cyclones, which is what hurricanes are called in this corner of the world. When you consider that most of the inhabitants of Vanuatu live in villages constructed of wood and thatch, where they survive largely through the cultivation of fruit trees and vegetable gardens, one can see how potentially devastating cyclones are for the islanders, or Ni-Vanuatu, as they are called. Not only can the typical Ni-Vanuatu depend on losing his home and livelihood during a cyclone; he can expect this to happen several times over the course of his life. Such is the world that nature has bequeathed to them. It did not surprise me, then, to learn that the water around Vanuatu is also shark-infested.

I recalled life in Kiribati, where every facet of existence was starkly shaped by the environment. It was very different from Washington, where nature had been reduced to just another trite political issue, and one's thoughts on the environment indicated whether one played for the blue team or the red team. On Tarawa, fish migrations determined what one had for dinner; a rain squall meant that, finally, there would be enough water to wash your hair; and the tides limited how far you could travel on the island. Life was reduced to its most elemental, and this, of course, affected the culture. Where I'm from, when we see a shark, we get out of the water. In Kiribati, when people see a shark, they gleefully dive in and try to catch it. Geography, as they say, is destiny.

Similarly, the isolated, trembling islands of Vanuatu, with their fire-breathing volcanoes and tempestuous cyclones, have produced a particularly intriguing culture uniquely adapted to the world they live in. During our time in Port Vila two years earlier, it seemed as if every Westerner we met was an anthropologist, freshly returned from the deepest, darkest bush, pith helmet in tow. It is no wonder. While the Ni-Vanuatu are Melanesian (Latin for "of the black islands"), descendants of intrepid voyagers who first sailed from Papua New Guinea and the Solomon Islands roughly four thousand years ago, they share little in common beyond appearance. Vanuatu is a country of chiefs and clans, each with unique traditions and beliefs. Some thought a bone through the nasal septum made them particularly fetching. Others manipulated the skulls of their infants until they became suitably elongated. As mentioned earlier, many Ni-Vanuatu men today wear nothing more than a *namba*, a modest leaf wrapped around their penis. Naturally, there are Big Nambas and Small Nambas. And they don't like each other.

Then there are the languages. The two hundred thousand people who call Vanuatu home speak more than one hundred languages. There is no place on Earth that offers more linguistic diversity. On some islands, and these are not large islands, the inhabitants will speak one of more than two dozen local languages, all unintelligible to one another. How can this be? you wonder. These people have been sharing an island—an island!—for a thousand years, or two, or four, and yet their languages have evolved utterly independent of those of their neighbors, a mere conch-shell blow away. Visiting the islands, one quickly understands that the topography certainly has something to do with it. The islands of Vanuatu are invariably rugged, as one would expect of islands prone to blowing up. And the interiors of most are forbiddingly dense with jungle. On Tanna, an island in the south, this area is known as the Middle Bush, an evocative name straight out of J. R. R. Tolkien. Mordor, if you will, can be found on the Ash Plain, where centuries of volcanic eruptions have decimated all life, leaving a gray, barren, and twisted landscape that fairly shouts DO NOT ENTER.

But, clearly, something else must have been afoot for so few people sharing so little land to speak so many languages. A quick glance at the early literature on Vanuatu provides a clue. The year 1893 saw the publication of the intriguing tome *Cannibals Won for Christ*, which was soon followed by *My Adventures Among South Sea Cannibals, From Fiji to the Cannibal Islands*, and 1922's seminal *Cannibal-land*. Colorful titles all—at least I certainly thought so. What the books so subtly referred to was the lusty appetites Vanuatu men had for other men. Cannibalism was rife in the islands, and that small fact, I deduced, was why the Ni-Vanuatu went to such trouble to avoid one another. Imagine, if you will, going for a stroll through the forest, where you chance upon a few men from the neighboring village. Elsewhere in the world, one might spend a couple of minutes idly talking about the weather, local politics, or real estate prices and then, with a friendly wave, wander on. Or perhaps you would ignore each other completely. In Vanuatu, however, you'd better run like hell, for if you were captured by your neighbors, you could be assured that, very shortly, you would be shat out their backsides.

Surely, you think, this was all a very long time ago. A century or two of contact with other cultures must undoubtedly have tempered habitual cannibalism. And it did, though not before scores of missionaries and sailors ended their days by stewing in a pot. But tradition has a way of hanging on. The last *officially recorded* incident of cannibalism in Vanuatu was in 1969 on the island of Malekula. I was born in 1969, and while I am willing to concede that 1969 is rapidly receding into the dim mists of time, it wasn't *that* long ago. Humor me. It seemed to me that if people were still officially gnawing at human limbs in 1969, it was more than possible that, since then, there had been some off-the-books cannibalism going on in Vanuatu. Our companions in Port Vila agreed. On Ambrym, they said. It's the island of black magic. Or on Malekula, particularly among the swaggering Big Nambas.

But, of course, it is not all cannibalism in Vanuatu. We are, after all, more than what we eat. On many islands, the inhabitants still live according to the tenets of *kastom,* the venerable traditions and beliefs that have infused Ni-Vanuatu culture since long before ships arrived from the West bearing muskets and missionaries. While the Ni-Vanuatu may have abandoned the consumption of human flesh, many still cling tenaciously to the old ways, in which the curve of a pig's tusk is of far greater value than the thinness of a flat-screen television. This is a world of spirits, magic, and sorcery, where an enemy can be slain with the right spell. But *kastom,* a pidgin word meaning "custom," manifests itself differently on each of the islands in Vanuatu. On Pentecost Island, for example, there are land divers, courageous boys and men who leap from homemade towers that soar upwards of ninety feet with nothing more than a vine tethered to their ankles, then plummet, grazing the hard earth with their hair, thus ensuring a successful yam harvest. On a few islands, however, the peculiarities of local culture have been infused with the peculiarities of the Western world, with the result that some villagers fly the U.S. Navy flag and march like American soldiers in the fervent hope that one day soon an enigmatic stranger will visit them bearing U.S. Army surplus material.

Yes, it is an odd country, made odder still by its colonial history. I had a hard time imagining the British and the French sharing anything but a healthy disregard for each other, but before Vanuatu's independence in 1980, the two countries jointly ruled the islands, which were then known as the New Hebrides, or Nouvelles-Hébrides, as the other half preferred. The two colonial powers spent the entire era, nearly a hundred years, crudely trying to undermine each other, with the result that today half the country is francophone while the other half leans anglophone—this in addition to the myriad indigenous languages. Naturally, for the Ni-Vanuatu to be able to communicate with anyone from outside their village, one more language had to be created: Bislama, an island pidgin. Mixing phonetic English with phonetic French, the Ni-Vanuatu now had a simple way to say "I don't understand": *Me no save.*

Thus, if ever there was a cure for urban ennui, Vanuatu was it. As I rode the subway around Washington, gathering what I thought we needed for our new lives—snorkels, flippers, spare flip-flops, sunscreen (family size)—I could barely contain my glee. Typically, I found riding the Metro during rush hour hypnotically depressing. For some reason it felt perceptibly different from riding the subways in New York, London, or Berlin. Elsewhere, one senses a certain liveliness, with people babbling to their neighbors, and at least a third of the passengers, perhaps even half, appearing rather pleased to be here, right now, with you, convivially sharing a subway car. On Washington's Red Line, which may as well be called the White Line as it rumbles below the city's palest quadrant, the atmosphere is discernibly different. It is all rustling of newspapers and ruffling of reports. It is sighing and harrumphing, little nonverbal gestures that say, all things being equal, they rather wish the entire world would

fuck off. Washingtonians, it occurred to me, were not flip-flop people. I wondered how different America would be if the capital had
been located in Key West. What if the nation's motto had been *Let's
get drunk and screw*? Would the world be a better place?

Such were my thoughts when the subway doors opened and on
hobbled a stunningly attractive woman. As a married man, I try
very hard not to be an ogre, but she possessed such beauty that I
couldn't help but furtively stare, even though she was nowhere near
as good looking as my wife, a point I'm adding here under no duress
whatsoever. Anyway, a real beauty she was. And tragically, she was in
a cast, which had the effect of accentuating her thigh, a description
of which I have been asked to remove. Now, if my sense of the male
condition is correct, and I'm fairly certain it is, one would expect
that on a crowded subway car the appearance of Aphrodite herself,
straining with her crutches, would lead to a near riot of men tripping over themselves to gallantly offer her a seat. But no such thing
happened. Instead, the papers were crisply rustled, and the men of
Washington returned to their stewing. I found this, frankly, astonishing, for not only were they being terrifically rude, but they were
also, evidently, eunuchs.

As the subway bounced along the tracks, I could see, to my considerable distress, that this poor woman was manifestly in pain. The
subway car swayed this way and that, and she winced, struggling to
hold herself upright. Beside her, comfortable in their seats, were two
men. The man on the outside seat appeared to be thirty-something,
besuited and balding, with the sort of gold-rimmed glasses that certain men wear to convey an appearance of wealth, though the effect
is usually one of premature aging. I watched him, just sitting there
mere inches from a woman standing with a broken leg, and I concluded that he was a cretin of the worst kind, and as I noted all the
other men seated in the subway car, including those occupying the

seats reserved for the elderly and the handicapped, this smug little puffin came to represent all that I found odious about Washington.

"Hey, man," I said to him. "Stand up and let the lady with the broken leg have a seat."

He looked, much to my gratification, as if he had just swallowed a lemon. His face began to contort as it tried to settle on an appropriate emotion. "How . . . who do you . . . ," he began to stammer. Then he thought better of it, and with considerable petulance, he rose.

"Thank you," said she of the golden smile. I tried to think of something witty to say, but one has only a moment and the moment passed, and I could think of nothing more than a bashful, blushing "You're welcome."

This wouldn't have happened in the South Pacific, I thought. Possibly because there weren't any subways in the South Pacific. As the train rumbled through the tunnel I reflected on the Pacific Islanders I had known. They might kill you because they thought you were practicing black magic. They might burn your house down because you inadvertently helped yourself to a coconut from a tree that had been deemed taboo. But they were never rude. Occasionally violent, yes. Emotionally unpredictable, sure. But always courteous. And frankly, I thought, the world could use a little more courtesy.

THERE ARE FEW sensations stranger than jet lag. For hour after hour you sit in an airplane doing nothing more taxing than reading a plot-driven novel, periodically eating, and perhaps, if you are very fortunate, even napping, and yet despite all this pampered nothingness, when you emerge from your airplane some hours later, you inevitably feel shattered. I can never quite understand it. Typically, I am awake for about seventeen hours a day. When I am employed, much of the day is occupied by work. If I am feeling particularly ambitious, I will use an hour to exercise. The rest of the day is spent in the usual manner, and after seventeen or so hours I may feel a little tired, a little groggy, and I call an end to the day. Put me on an airplane for seventeen hours, however, and I feel as if I've just completed the Bataan Death March.

"So this is New Zealand?" I said to Sylvia as we found ourselves standing on a curb at Auckland Airport.

"It's cold," Sylvia noted.

"And gray," I added.

"Very wet also."

"We'll have to come back one day," I said. And then we turned around, marched back into the terminal, and caught the flight to Vanuatu. Five hours later, we found ourselves on the curb at Bauerfield International Airport, a few miles outside Port Vila, on the island of Efate. What a long, strange day it's been, I thought as I wrestled with our luggage, sweating freely in the heat. When I woke up the previous morning, I had been on the other side of the planet. And now here I was on an island in the South Pacific. Look, palm trees. Were those parrots? And hey, everyone's African American. No, not African American. Melanesian. Where am I?

Sometimes, when traveling long distances, it feels as if you have hardly moved at all, that you have simply exchanged the white noise of home for the same noise spoken in a different language. Not so in Vanuatu. The islands feel satisfyingly far away, like Lilliputian planets inhabiting the bluest of universes, distant places where, as we enviously took note of the airport workers snoozing in the afternoon shade, there is always time for a nap.

But not for us. Not yet. Still stupefied by jet lag, we soon found ourselves in the spirited company of Rex, Sylvia's new boss, a Solomon Islander who had once served as his country's representative to the United Nations in New York. That evening, he very kindly hosted a dinner for us at his airy home, of which, alas, I have only the barest of memories. Exhaustion combined with a glass of wine or two does not do wonders for my sociability. I dimly recall an animated discussion about the situation in Fiji that ended with me lying supine on his couch, from which, no doubt, I charmed my fellow guests with the occasional, gasping snort. Somehow, and probably with much relief, we were deposited in a motel room, where we slept for fourteen hours straight under the crisp whir of a ceiling fan.

"Did I utterly embarrass myself last night?" I asked Sylvia when we awoke the next day.

"I have no memory of last night," she said.

"Probably just as well."

So it was a surprise when Kathy, another of Sylvia's colleagues, arrived at the motel with her SUV. Evidently, we had made arrangements the previous evening to borrow her truck and go rambling around the island. This struck us as a very agreeable way to begin our stay in Vanuatu, and we were pleased that we had thought of it, though a little befuddled that we had not remembered.

"Just be really careful," Kathy warned us. "It rained a couple of days ago, so the road is likely to be dangerous."

"Don't worry," I said. "While it may be true that I have never in thirty-some years of life actually owned a car, I assure you that I am an excellent driver."

"You've lived in America for most of your life and never owned a car?"

"Or driven an SUV," I added happily. She gave a nervous twitch, but I pried the keys out of her hand, and soon we were off, tires squealing. It was a bewilderingly odd sensation. One day we were shuffling about Washington, D.C., quietly contemptuous of our surroundings, and a day or so later, here we were on faraway Vanuatu, driving a large sport utility vehicle. This was dissonance at its best.

Within moments, we had put the paved roads of Port Vila behind us and begun our cautious circumnavigation of Efate, following a sixty-mile-long, deeply gutted dirt road that meandered around the island. Port Vila, we had already discerned, was an island within an island. It had electricity, stores, restaurants, and resorts. There was even a disco. But the moment one left the town limits, it was the raw Pacific that beckoned. Very often the road would narrow into a bush trail before suddenly widening into enormous mud pits where bulldozers stood idle and empty, parked in a remarkably haphazard fashion, as if they were forgotten remnants of some long-ago road-improvement project. The signs read COURTESY OF THE GOVERNMENT OF JAPAN. Otherwise, the road was barren of vehicles, which was just as well, for despite being in a four-wheel drive, I frequently found myself wildly fishtailing across the mud.

"Just tap the breaks," Sylvia suggested helpfully.

"That's what I'm doing. But if you'd like, you can drive."

Sylvia shook her head. "I have to work with Kathy. If we're going to crash her truck, it's better that you do it."

I had no intention of crashing someone else's truck, so we moseyed on as prudently as we could. Efate, we could see, was a dauntingly lush island with a jungle that toppled over steep hillsides, much of it enveloped with the mile-a-minute vine planted by the Americans in World War II—camouflage run amok. Along the shore, there were coconut plantations and a couple of cattle ranches, where cows idled under massive banyan trees. Life on the isle, the human kind, was also largely found on the fringes. In the few somnolent villages we passed through, there were small kiosks made of clapboard and tin with shelves offering vegetables, seashells, and sixty-year-old Coke bottles for sale. Payments could be dropped inside the Honesty Box. And all along there was the ocean, the South Pacific, majestic and beguiling.

"Where is everyone?" I wondered as I deposited a few coins inside the Honesty Box in exchange for a couple of green coconuts. We were in a small seaside village. To our Western eyes, it looked very poor, with homes made of wood, thatch, and corrugated tin and gardens encased by rickety chicken-wire fences. But one's sense of poverty becomes skewed in moving so quickly from America, where technically most people are hundreds of thousands of dollars in debt and even the poor have televisions, to a place like Vanuatu, where wealth is measured in pig tusks.

"I think it might be Sunday," Sylvia said as she used our Swiss Army knife to carve holes into her coconut like an old Pacific hand. At some point in our journey, we had crossed the international date line, that imaginary line where today becomes tomorrow, and the moment you were experiencing just a moment ago is now, apparently, a couple of days behind you. Or something like that. We stood for a long while, puzzling through the complexity of time, and just as our brains began to hurt, we heard hymns emanating from the tin-roofed church just up the road. Sunday it was.

"No wonder there's no one else on the road," I said. Not all Ni-Vanuatu are Christian, of course, though Efate, as the most Westernized island in Vanuatu, has largely been converted. On the outer islands, many retain the old ways and follow the dictates of kastom. How traditional they actually were was something I planned on exploring. Others belonged to cargo cults, eagerly awaiting the day when fortune would smile and illuminate their lives with tinned Spam and revolvers, the detritus of World War II. But as elsewhere in the South Pacific, for the Christians in Vanuatu, Sundays were for devotion. There is no quieter place on Earth than a Pacific island on a Sunday. Unless you venture inside a church. When it comes to singing, Pacific Islanders would give Southern Baptists a run for their money.

We continued on our excursion, and the farther we traveled from Port Vila, the more treacherous the road became. After a rather exhilarating slide down a hill with my foot pressing the brake as far as it would go, we probably ought to have listened to our more sensible instincts and turned around. We drove on, however, partly because I am constitutionally incapable of backtracking, but mostly because the scenery was so alluring and each curve and every crest promised another vista of paradise. There were coconut palms with their fronds moving like languorous fans, and I was feeling tremendously pleased to be among them again. The hillsides were impressively dense and green, exuding an air of primordial wilderness. Those woods, I had read, contained a multitude of lizards, including the banded iguana, a fearsome-looking dragon that grows upwards of three feet in length. There was also the Pacific boa, an eight-foot-long snake that I hoped never to encounter. It is said that the Pacific boa is harmless, but I didn't believe that for a moment. Raised as a Catholic, I still find it difficult to have warm and mushy feelings toward snakes. We stopped here and there, never encountering another vehicle, and listened to the quiet buzz of insects and the lazy calls of birds slumbering in the midday sun. There was a torporous serenity to the island, and the lingering small pressures that remained of our lives in Washington, the urge to hurry on, to check e-mail, to do errands, evaporated with the rising heat.

On the north shore of Efate, the views took a sudden turn toward the dramatic. There, offshore, were the volcanic islands of Nguna, Pele, and Emao, and farther in the distance, the Shepherd Islands, jagged green domes that rose precipitously out of the sea, the only visible remnants of a single island, Kuwae, that exploded—as islands in Vanuatu are wont to do—in a titanic fifteenth-century volcanic eruption. What remained of the island soon receded into the sea, leaving only the crests that today constitute the Shepherd Islands.

Remarkably, local legends spoke of one man who survived the catastrophe, Ti Tongoa Liseiriki, who, when he died, was buried wearing three round pig tusks around his arm. Even today, curved pig tusks are highly prized in Vanuatu, much to the consternation of the islands' pig community. The tusks curve after a pig's upper teeth have been yanked out. Subsequently, the animal must be fed by hand. The tusks continue to curve until they loop back through the snout and upper jaw, completing the circle. A really unfortunate pig will finds its tusks completing two or, very rarely, three complete circles as its owner celebrates his good fortune. The possessor of a triple-circle tusk is a wealthy man in Vanuatu. Less valuable than the pig tusks, however, were the wives and many of the men who had proclaimed fealty to Ti Tongoa Liseiriki. They too were buried alongside him. All had been killed for the occasion. In the 1960s, a French archeologist, José Garanger, took heed of the legend and, shovel in hand, proceeded to dig up Mr. Liseiriki, complete with pig tusks and entourage.

This wasn't the only legend Monsieur Garanger chose to investigate in this corner of Vanuatu. There was also the tale of Roy Mata, a chief who counted northern Efate and the Shepherd Islands as his domain. In the mid-thirteenth century, Roy Mata—just Roy to his friends—violently conquered the region, and once he was recognized as the preeminent chief, he very sensibly declared that henceforth warfare would be forbidden. Every five years his subordinate chiefs held a grand feast to celebrate the peace, which endured for a long fifteen years until, very sadly for the chiefs, Roy Mata was poisoned, presumably by his brother, who is believed to have been called Gary. While this intrigue was as compelling as any that occurred among the kings of medieval Europe, its ending was uniquely macabre. It was said that upon the death of Roy Mata, his eighteen loyal subservient chiefs joined him in the grave, where, fortified by a particularly strong brew of kava, Vanuatu's favorite narcotic beverage, the men awaited their end. Joined by their twenty-two wives, who had been strangled to death, the chiefs were buried alive. The grave, on Eretoka Island, was declared taboo. Hearing of this legend, Garanger brought his shovel to Eretoka, where he soon found a grave with forty-one skeletons, including one bejeweled with pig tusks, an obviously high-ranking chief who could only have been Roy Mata.

I mention these disturbing details because if you ever happen to find yourself on north Efate—particularly at the small cove we found, where the water lapped gently against a glorious white sand beach, and in the near distance a small fringing reef captured the ocean swell, and a little farther on a couple of perfect green islets framed the vast, astonishingly blue South Pacific—you will be very hard-pressed to imagine that anything even remotely dark or cruel or gruesome could possibly occur in such an Edenic setting. Certainly, no such thoughts occurred to us.

"Let's go for a swim," I said to Sylvia a tad impulsively.

"I didn't bring a swimsuit."

"It's Sunday. Who cares?"

Well, perhaps the Ni-Vanuatu Christians would have cared. But we knew where they were, and so we celebrated creation in our own way, in the buff, with a delightful swim in the mild waters of the South Seas. It was like a baptism of sorts, a chance to wash off the sins of office life and begin anew. I couldn't think of a better way to resume our island existence than to spend a Sunday afternoon cavorting in the tranquil waters of a protected cove, somewhere off an island on the far side of the world. It didn't occur to us then that this was a reckless and foolhardy thing to do. Vanuatu is notorious for shark attacks, and to tempt fate by swimming near a reef without first enquiring about the resident shark population is exceedingly rash and ill-advised. For all we knew, the local name for this beach might have been Place Where Many Large Sharks Come to Feed on Stupid Naked Tourists. Happily, though, our swim went uncontested by large sea critters, and we settled into the kind of mirth that occurs when, after a long spell elsewhere, you suddenly find yourself in a good, good place.

"I could live here," Sylvia said.

"And now you do." I smiled.

As we hopped back into the truck we were feeling immoderately satisfied with ourselves. We had done it, escaped the proverbial rat race and its ceaseless hustle and bustle and exchanged that world for one where, we hoped, we would once again live as contented exiles, modern Crusoes, finding gratification in the small pleasures life offers, like languid dips in the temperate waters of the South Pacific Ocean. It was perhaps inevitable, then, that a short while later we found ourselves back in the truck and gasping theatrically as we slipped down a perilously steep incline, the wheels locked in place by the foot brake, then by the hand brake—and yet still we could not halt the descent. Looming at the bottom was a glade of coconut trees, and those trees, I could see, were not going anywhere.

"Brake!" Sylvia yelled.

The mud-slicked road curved around the trees. Straining to control the truck as it slid toward its seemingly inevitable collision, I released the brakes, pressed the gas with as much confidence as I could muster, swung the wheel around the curve, and then immediately felt a sickening panic as the back wheels proceeded around in a graceless arc, up and over the road embankment, and with a shocking thud we found ourselves implanted upon a berm of mud.

"Well," I said once my heart had slowed, "on the plus side, we're alive."

"On the down side, we're stuck," Sylvia noted.

"Not necessarily." I gave the gas an optimistic tap, and as I felt the truck begin to shudder, I pressed the pedal more firmly, whereupon I noticed to my dismay that the back of the truck was discernibly sinking ever deeper into the mud. I took my foot off the gas. "Now we're stuck."

We spent a long, silent moment absorbing the situation. This was the most remote corner of Efate. We were miles and miles of hard trekking from the nearest village. We had not seen another vehicle all day, and it being Sunday, we were unlikely to encounter one until the following day. We had, very possibly, damaged someone else's truck. We were stuck in mud.

"Don't you just hate it when good days go bad," I said.

With sighs of resignation, we opened the doors and plopped down into the mud, a viscous, gooey mass of brown slime that embraced us up to our shins. The back wheels were deeply implanted, and even more worrying was the ridge of thick mud and rock upon which the truck's frame rested, with the front wheels only lightly grazing the ground. It was eerily quiet, even the birds and bugs choosing to remain silent in the midafternoon heat. We suddenly felt very much alone, far removed from everything except our problem.

There was nothing else to do but to start digging. From either side of the truck, we attacked the berm with our hands, scraping aside the mire, flinging most of it upon ourselves.

"You look like the Creature from the Black Lagoon," Sylvia commented a short while later as we took a short break from our excavations.

"You should talk."

Soon, we were both encrusted in thick layers of primeval muck that oozed as it mixed with rivulets of sweat. As we drained the contents of our last remaining water bottle, flies appeared, seemingly out of nowhere, and soon they began to pester us with shocking rapacity. We returned to our digging, periodically pausing to slap ourselves senseless in a futile effort at murdering these swarms of misery. I resolved that if we ever had children, I would show them how amusing it is to pluck the wings off flies.

After much effort, the rear wheels were cleared of about as much mud and debris as we could manage, and I set about foraging for fallen coconut fronds, hoping that they could provide sufficient traction for us to extract the truck. Stepping into the crunchy detritus of fallen leaves and branches, I noticed an assortment of small lizards scattering hither and thither, and it was only with determined effort that I managed to refrain from hightailing it up a tree. What a pansy-ass city boy I had become in Washington, I thought. I wondered if there might be a large boa constrictor lurking underfoot, just waiting for a serendipitous encounter, and shuddered grimly at the thought. Soon, however, as I pulled a few long fronds toward the truck, it was the mosquitoes that were driving me toward the brink. The buzz in my ears was followed by the ringing of my ears as I battered myself in a hopeless quest to stem my blood loss. With each puncture, a dozen flies would feed on the welt, leaving me stewing and foaming, quietly muttering, *fucking tropics.*

"Are you being attacked by mosquitoes?" I asked Sylvia.

"Yes," she said, "which is why I'm going to sit inside the truck now."

"Ah . . . perhaps you'd like to turn on the air conditioner too, maybe find something pleasant to listen to on the radio, perhaps read a magazine."

"My thinking exactly."

"Just one question before you retire. Is there malaria on Efate?"

"Only on north Efate."

"I see . . . But we're on north Efate."

"Which is why I'm going to sit inside the truck now."

Sylvia closed the door with a satisfied thud. Then she rolled down the window. "I've decided that getting a truck out of the mud is man's work."

"Have you now?"

"Yes. And see, you're a man, so I think it's very simple." And with that she rolled up the window.

Why was it, I wondered, that this was always a one-way conversation. How come *You're the woman. Now go get me a beer* never worked. But *You're the man. It's your job to fix the faucet, mow the lawn, get the truck out of the mud,* and so on was always greeted with a stoic acknowledgment of one's duty and a solemn commitment to do what needs to be done sometime very soon, possibly tomorrow even. It was entirely unjust. Nevertheless, I returned to my manly obligations and confidently placed the fronds under the rear wheels. I tapped on the window.

"Sorry to disturb you, but if it's not too much trouble, would you mind terribly putting the truck into gear and, at my say-so, giving it a bit of gas?"

Sylvia chuckled. "No, I wouldn't mind at all."

I positioned myself behind the truck, slapped a few flies and mosquitoes off my face, and fervently hoped that in a few short minutes I too would be allowed inside the truck, task accomplished. I sought some leverage by placing a foot against a rock, leaned into the truck, and said, "Okay. Now!"

Sylvia floored it. The wheels spun wildly, and if we had happened to be on a paved road, we would have undoubtedly been moving at well over one hundred miles per hour. But since we were not on a paved road but on a berm of mud, I saw, to my consternation, that the truck was in fact sliding ever farther backward. I heaved with all my might. The palm fronds splintered into nothingness. The spinning wheels dug through layers of mud, spraying a brown mist deep into the bush. I took my foot off the rock, and then my flip-flops lost all traction. "BRAKE! BRAKE! BRAKE!" I yelled as a ton of steel pushed at me with incontestable momentum.

A moment later I was in the passenger seat, panting from the exertion. I turned the air conditioner to its highest setting. "So, how long have we been in Vanuatu now?"

"A little less than twenty-four hours," Sylvia answered.

We looked at each other, noted the streaming sweat, the mottled hair, the strata of grime, and the innumerable mosquito welts, and agreed that maybe we should have spent the day at a hotel pool, lounging and imbibing froufrou drinks.

"What do we do now?" Sylvia asked.

"Well," I said, looking a little more closely at our map, "I think we're about ten kilometers from the next village. We have, what, three, four hours left before darkness? We should probably start walking. We'll at least be able to find some water and food there. And we'll probably have to spend the night. There might be a guesthouse."

Before setting out, we crossed the road—or the big pile of sopping mud that was euphemistically called a road—and wandered toward the nearby ocean. There was, alas, no beach, just cragged ridges of rock absorbing the hard impact of a heaving ocean. It was much too rough for swimming, and we stumbled about in search of a tidal pool, hoping to cleanse ourselves of our filth. We found one and, mindful of the crabs and urchins, we swabbed ourselves clean, ignoring the sting of salt water flushing our mosquito bites.

"I hear something," Sylvia said, cocking her ear toward the road. "What?"

"A car . . . no, a truck."

It was unmistakable, the muddled grind of a large diesel engine straining in the mire. We dashed across the rock, throwing prudence to the wind, and as we reached the road we saw the aged dump truck coming from the opposite direction from whence we came. Here was something that could salvage us from our predicament. Sylvia stood in the middle of the road and proceeded to do what appeared to be very spirited jumping jacks, complete with flopping ponytail.

"I think he sees you," I said.

"Just making sure."

The truck grinded to a stop. In the back hold there were several dozen people dressed for church. The men had shirts on, and the women wore prim Mother Hubbards, one-piece frocks that were highly recommended by nineteenth-century missionaries. They smiled warmly at us. The driver, a stout, bearded fellow with an opaque expression, emerged from the cab and proceeded to say something. I had no idea what he was saying but recognized the language as Bislama. I recalled what I had learned during my first trip to Vanuatu and, using every word I had gleaned back then, said, "Me no tok-tok Bislama . . . uh . . . truck . . . uh, problemo . . . bugger up . . . Do you speak English?"

"Non," he said. "Je parle français."

"Excellent," I said. "Je parle français très bon."

As a child in Canada I had attended a bilingual school, which would have been very useful if I had remained in Canada, but I didn't, and ever since then I had been wondering when exactly my French skills, which I thought considerable, would ever be brought to use. Sylvia, however, who had lived in France, wasn't quite as confident in my French as I was, and after watching me struggle to find the exact bons mots to describe our predicament, she proceeded to engage the driver with an animated summation of our woes. As I listened I was willing to concede that her French was a little more *très bon* than mine, but what I found more remarkable was the fluency of the truck driver. We could not possibly be farther from France than we were in Vanuatu, and yet here was an indigenous islander speaking French with the refinement of a Parisian. I am never surprised anymore when I hear someone speak English. It is, these days, everyone's second language. But when I hear an Indonesian speak Dutch or a Mozambican utter Portuguese or a Ni-Vanuatu truck driver holding forth in French, I am always astonished at the reach and sweep of colonialism. This thought was further impressed upon me by the sight of several Melanesian women descending from the truck bed wearing the sort of frocks typically worn by Amish women in Pennsylvania. The colonists themselves, of course, had moved on to string bikinis and Speedos, but on Efate the islanders retained the stern modesty imposed by missionaries a century ago. I resolved that if ever we did go skinny-dipping again, we should do so only on a kastom island, where the Ni-Vanuatu had greeted the missionaries' austere dictates by eating them.

"He's got a chain," Sylvia said with undisguised glee a few minutes later. "He can tow us out."

"Pas de problème," the bearded man said.

I nearly kissed him, in the French way, but he wisely moved on, leaving us to mingle with his curious passengers. They were Catholics returning from a church service in the next village. I apologized for delaying their return home with our troubles, but they didn't seem to mind, though one effervescent young woman gently noted that one must be careful when driving on the road. I wanted to point out that in my country we wouldn't call this a road. We would call it mud and leave it at that. But it seemed impolite, and the conversation moved on to the only topic that mattered in the Pacific: How many children did we have? When we explained that we didn't have any, a heavy gloom descended, and sensing the sadness and woe—in the Pacific, there is no greater tragedy than a childless couple—we hastened to add that we hoped to start a family very soon, possibly here in Vanuatu. This lifted everyone's spirits, but the pity they felt for us was palpable.

By this time, the men had attached a chain connecting the two vehicles, and I left Sylvia to be soothed and comforted by the women while I sought to somehow make myself useful. This was difficult, since I have no particular aptitude for the mechanical realm. When I hear words such as *transmission* or *carburetor,* my brain immediately shuts down, as if it were encased behind thick steel trapdoors, where it sits idly protecting itself from any knowledge pertaining to cars. I shifted around, gave a thoughtful tug at the chain, nodded in satisfaction, furrowed my brow in concentration, and otherwise pretended to have vast amounts of experience pulling SUVs out of the mud. The truck driver started his engine, which began emitting powerful vroom-vrooms, and he leaned out the window, watching me with a cryptic expression.

"Nous sommes près, monsieur," he said.

Great, I thought. Right. Well. Carry on, if you please. I crossed my arms and beheld the scene with what I hoped was the detached professionalism of a tow-truck driver. Any moment now, the SUV would leap forth from the mire. Yes, any moment now . . . but the driver was still studying me with anticipation.

I should be doing something, I knew, but what? I tried to think logically. The big truck is going to pull the little truck. It seemed straightforward enough. Ah . . . might be a good idea to release the hand brake. With some sheepishness, I hopped inside the SUV and released the brake. What else should I do? I wondered. Put it in neutral? Start it and put it in gear? Yes, probably. Couldn't hurt? Could it?

I started the SUV and put it in first gear. The two trucks were nose to nose, about fifteen feet apart, and as I felt the tension in the chain I stepped on the gas. The big truck slowly pulled backward, and I felt the SUV grinding over the berm. The wheels spun freely in the gunk until traction was reclaimed, then suddenly and rather exhilaratingly, the SUV plowed forward, now released from the mud, and sped headlong toward the heavy truck. I slammed on the brakes, and in the long second that followed, it occurred to me that this would be one of the more unfortunate ways to wreck a vehicle, a brief moment of freedom followed by the clash of metal. It was only when the SUV had come to a stop mere inches from the front fender of the truck that I felt relief, knowing that there was still a chance to return the SUV to its owner in one piece.

I thanked the truck driver effusively for his help, noting the amusement of the onlookers, and soon we were on our way, continuing our circumnavigation of the island at a cautious three miles an hour. Sylvia was very pleased. A ten-kilometer hike in search of water and shelter, under an unrelenting swarm of flies and mosquitoes, followed by a debilitating bout of malaria was not how she had envisioned beginning our lives in Vanuatu.

"It's nice like this," she said as we rolled along a road that became progressively smoother as we neared Port Vila. The afternoon light had softened, and the colors of the island assumed a depth of intensity not found outside the tropics. We drove parallel with a long white-sand beach. The tide was in over the reef shelf, and in the distance the breakers seemed to stretch like long, unbroken lines of ivory streamers. Soon the dense forest gave way to verdant pastures where clusters of cattle, pure descendents of a French herd prized for their tender meat, milled about in the doleful manner of cows everywhere. There were signs now pointing the way to places of interest for tourists—a beach club, white-water rafting, horseback riding—and we were very happy to find ourselves on a paved road that took us past the gated homes of expatriates and the sprawling Le Meridien resort until we crested a couple of hills and found the turnoff to Elluk, the prosperous neighborhood where Kathy had a house overlooking Erakor Bay and the shimmering Pacific Ocean.

Settling comfortably on Kathy's verandah with a bottle of Tusker, the national beer, I decided that I liked Efate very much. Kathy was nonplussed by our misadventures with her SUV. "It happens to everyone," she said, very gracefully I thought. Indeed, she even offered to lend us her vehicle again whenever we might have need of it. She was from Pennsylvania originally, and after twenty years in the South Pacific, she had clearly adopted the tropical temperament: Stuff happens, but tomorrow the sun will rise again. Below us, bathed in the golden hues of sunset, the catamarans that belonged to the Crowne Plaza resort were being towed back to the shore by the hotel staff, who had raced across Erakor Lagoon in open boats with outboard engines. One sensed that this was an evening ritual for them, rescuing tourists from themselves. Elsewhere on the water, the local boys had taken out a few outrigger canoes, which they were gleefully using as diving platforms, and their shrills of laughter suggested an enviable boyhood. A pontoon boat weaved around them as it ferried passengers to the Erakor Island Resort; both the boys and the tourists waved, and one sensed that they were genuinely happy to see each other.

It seemed, for the moment, that Efate was about as agreeable an island as one could find, a perfect blending of worlds, where the comfort of the West mixed easily with the raw beauty of the tropics, and though I knew that this was a naïve and silly thought, I voiced it anyway, possibly because I was on my second Tusker.

"Well," Kathy said, "it's a great view from here, but don't be fooled by it. The government is incredibly corrupt here. Malaria is a huge problem on the outer islands. Literacy rates are among the lowest in the Pacific. The status of women here is just a fraction higher than that of pigs. And crime is a big problem in Port Vila."

I had figured as much. I wasn't a greenhorn anymore in these parts. Our two years on an atoll had shattered the illusion of island life. But I was fond of illusion.

"It's a great view, though."

The hills and the islands and the sea were bathed in a crimson twilight.

"It's the most beautiful view in the world," Kathy said.

CHAPTER 3

In which the author is confounded by Port Vila, which is not at all like the South Pacific he has known—he does not, for instance, have to eat fish every day—and after dipping into the past, which strikes him as being uncannily like the present, he cannot help but feel that for the whites in Vila it's forever 1900.

WHEN PAUL THEROUX, THE WORLD'S GREATEST LIVING Travel Writer, visited Port Vila some years ago to gather material for a book about the South Pacific, he stopped by the local library on Father Lini Highway, the two-lane road that carves through the town's center, and discovered, to his evident pleasure, that the stacks were flush with his books. I know this because shortly after we arrived in Port Vila, I too could be found inside the library, idly perusing the scattering of books written by Theroux, one of which was *The Happy Isles of Oceania*. I opened it up, turned to his chapter on Vanuatu, and read his account of visiting the library in Port Vila, which left me feeling very happy indeed, for here I was now, doing exactly what Paul Theroux was doing: standing in a library looking at the books written by Paul Theroux. This pleased me immensely. Theroux didn't have much else to say about Port Vila, and he soon moved on to Tanna Island, where he engaged in an epic battle with fire-and-brimstone Christian missionaries. I couldn't blame him. For itinerant travel writers, Port Vila is the worst kind of place. It is captivatingly pleasant.

Appealingly situated on rolling hills, offering vistas over the bays and lagoons that jabbed the island like impertinent fingers, Port Vila is quite likely the finest town of its size in the South Pacific. Admittedly, this is saying very little. It isn't as if the islands are graced with their own Pragues and Romes, but then again, neither Prague nor Rome has palm-fringed beaches. Oceania is a world of villages, each with its own rules and routines. And with strikingly few exceptions, the larger urban areas like Port Moresby in Papua New Guinea are either cesspools of criminality or dissolute slums like South Tarawa in Kiribati, where the inhabitants drift ever further from the village culture that has sustained them for generations. Port Vila, then, is an agreeable anomaly in the South Pacific. It's nice.

It wasn't always so. Like all large towns in the region, Port Vila is a town built by Westerners for Westerners. Indeed, until the 1940s, the Ni-Vanuatu were not even allowed to live in Vila, as the locals call their town. Any Ni-Vanuatu men found wandering about after 9 P.M. were arrested. This, remarkably, was an improvement over the state of affairs that prevailed in the 1880s, when Port Vila was little more than a debauched port for planters, beachcombers, ex-convicts, and blackbirders—rapacious labor recruiters who plied the South Pacific, filling their holds with bodies to send to plantations and mines throughout the Southern Hemisphere. One hotel in particular came to be known as the "bloodhouse." R. J. Fletcher in *Isles of Illusion* (published in 1925) described an evening at the inn:

> *I have seen recruiters playing poker after a successful season. The drink is champagne . . . ordered in cases. The regulation method is to shout for a case, kick the lid off and open the bottles with an 18″ knife. The stakes are merely the recruited niggers who are ranged solemnly around the wall of the room and change hands many times a night.*

*Fancy the excitement of a jackpot of four stalwart niggers and two
women (total value 92 pounds) in the pool.*

It is difficult to imagine what Vanuatu must have been like in the
nineteenth century, when everyone from unscrupulous sandalwood
traders to zealous missionaries began to appear, uninvited of
course, on islands whose inhabitants had developed a fine appreciation for the culinary possibilities of human flesh. The Ni-Vanuatu
ate a good many of the foreigners among them, but it wasn't long
before the tide had turned and settlers could be found posting signs
that said DOGS AND NIGGERS ARE FORBIDDEN TO ENTER INSIDE THE
PORTALS OF THESE GATES. ANY DOGS OR NIGGERS FOUND THEREIN
WILL SUFFER THE PENALTY OF DEATH.

The settlers were just as charming toward other settlers. By the
turn of the century, there were 55 British settlers and 151 French.
"We have just celebrated Christmas," wrote one observer in 1888,
"and Christmas in the New Hebrides is a fearful and wonderful
sight. Thank God it only comes once a year. The French and the
English had a pitched battle but luckily they were all too drunk to
shoot straight." Port Vila's days as a distant backwater eventually
took a turn toward the farcical with the establishment of the Anglo-
French Condominium, one of history's more peculiar colonial
arrangements. This joint rule represented an attempt by the British
and French governments to restore some order to the islands. The
Condominium, which was established in 1906, could best be described as a petulant compromise between the French and the English. Anyone who has ever watched two cranky toddlers argue over
an Etch A Sketch can envision the result. *You can't have it,* said the
French, who wanted to annex the New Hebrides to settle their ex-
convicts from New Caledonia. *Well, you can't have it either,* said the
English. England, of course, couldn't have cared less about the New

Hebrides, but its little brother Australia did, and so the Condominium was proclaimed. The French busily drew plans for the islands, and then the English erased those plans and created their own, which were then scribbled over by the French, and so on, until finally, exasperated, the two countries drew a line down the middle of the Etch A Sketch. The result was two high commissions, two governments, two official ruling languages, two flags that competed for the loftiest perch, two currencies, two postage stamps, and two educational systems. Depending on where they lived, the Ni-Vanuatu found themselves inhabiting a world that leaned either anglophone or francophone, and each group was told to mistrust the other. As one can imagine, this did nothing for the subsequent stability of independent Vanuatu. In any given year, the government is likely to change as the francophones topple an anglophone government, who then spend their time plotting to remove the francophones, and so on. On the bright side, in Port Vila one can now begin one's day with a flaky croissant and a steaming bowl of café au lait and end it with a heaping platter of fish and chips washed down with a frothy pint of lager.

Today, some thirty thousand people live in Vila, and while the vast majority are Ni-Vanuatu, the atmosphere, by Pacific standards, is decidedly cosmopolitan. The center of town reflects a fading colonial heritage and a rising future in banking. There are fifty-five banks in Port Vila. As far as I could tell, only three were banks in the traditional sense, bricks-and-mortar buildings containing vaults and money and tellers and ATMs. The other fifty-two banks were a little more ephemeral. Vanuatu is a tax haven. Inevitably every year or so, it is listed as one of the top ten go-to destinations for money launderers and tax evaders. This confers a certain air of intrigue to Port Vila. Sitting in a café, I'd find myself wondering about the man at the next table, reclining there with his pipe and briefcase, picking

at his croque monsieur. A missionary? Or an international super-
criminal?

One tends not to think of the South Pacific as a particularly diverse place. People tend to be attracted to the center of things, and
no region is more peripheral. Yet, in Port Vila, one finds a town inhabited by daring French fashionistas clicking down the sidewalks
in designer heels alongside plump Melanesian women in modest
flower-print Mother Hubbards. There are Australian tourists, all
inexplicably wearing cornrows on reddened scalps, wandering
through the covered market alongside ink-dark, barefoot men from
the outer islands. Every couple of weeks, a cruise ship disgorges
a thousand gaping visitors, who spend their day in Vanuatu buying
trinkets in the market and perfume in the duty-free shops, but
mostly drinking beer, before returning to their ship and continuing
on their journey exploring the sights and sounds of the South Seas.
There are also semi-tame frontier men from the Australian outback
who have settled in Port Vila, where they pass their evenings at the
pub complaining about what a good-for-nothing dirty sod your
Ni-Van is, as all the while their Ni-Vanuatu girlfriends twitter beside
them. There are Chinese merchants who have established a veritable
mini-Chinatown on the streets above Father Lini Highway. There is
a Vietnamese community, descendents of Tonkinese laborers recruited by the French to work the coconut plantations. And there
are the missionaries, in town for a few days, splurging on lemon-
ades, awaiting a flight to the outer islands, where they will try to
convince the many who retain kastom ways that they really, really
need to put some clothes on.

During our first few weeks in Port Vila, we simply absorbed this
odd tableau. From the terrace of Le Café du Village, a dockside
restaurant where we'd linger after sumptuous seafood meals, there
was an appealing view of the harbor, with several dozen sailboats

anchored in the safety between town and nearby Iririki Island, a green-domed isle that in colonial times served as the home of the British high commissioner and now held a high-end resort. Since we were now in the summer months—a relative term, of course, in the South Pacific—the sailboats were riding out the cyclone season in the splendid shelter of Vila Harbor before moving on in their rambling journeys to who knows where. Graybeards, I called their captains, for nearly to a man they sported proud whiskers. There must have been a rule about it, I figured, one decreeing that men sailing the South Seas are required to look like dissolute buccaneers. One Frenchman, who was refurbishing his two-master for the entertainment of the diners at the Waterfront Bar and Grill—or so it seemed to me—wore a resplendent white beard, a braided ponytail, and a golden loop in his ear (to pay for his funeral, of course), and spent his days ambling up and down his gangplank, flexing his tattoos, wondering how he might be able to say *Argh, matey* in French. During the sailing season, the harbor was dense with boats from New Caledonia, a French colony about a three-day sail away, and the colonists from New Caledonia would spend their days pretending to be colonists from Vanuatu, barking orders at waitresses and maids.

It wasn't long before I began to envy the yachties. The ones who had crossed an ocean or two invariably had boats notable not only for their size but for their homeyness. And well they might, since for many of the yachties their boats were the only home they had. It had taken us the better part of a month to find a house to rent. This is because Port Vila is an astonishingly expensive place to live. We had thought, foolishly perhaps, that as Westerners with Western money, we would be able to afford a relatively sumptuous abode, a house with a view and a garden, we hoped. Vanuatu, after all, is one of the poorest countries on earth, with a per capita income of about $700 per year. Surely, we thought, the cost of living would reflect that.

And so when Madame Poiret, a real-estate agent and property manager, began to show us the homes available for rent, we sputtered in disbelief as we contemplated paying the equivalent of our rent in Washington for a derelict cinder-block structure just one small earthquake away from collapsing down a steep cliff.

"Le paradis est cher," said Madame Poiret, dragging on a cigarette. I hadn't been in Port Vila long enough to determine whether this was paradise. But it was certainly expensive. We were trying, uncharacteristically, to be fiscally prudent. I had invested the money I'd saved from my time at the World Bank, and being a savvy investor, I had put most of it in tech stocks. I had one year, one last year, to write a book that someone would buy, and in the meantime, we planned to live off Sylvia's salary. Eventually, we swallowed hard and moved into a small bungalow that offered a sweeping view of Vila Harbor. Of course, between the house and the view there stood a three-story apartment building. We couldn't afford the million-dollar view, but if we stood on chairs, which we did daily, we'd just manage to see the waters of Mele Bay and the verdant hillsides that stretched toward Devil's Point. It was a modest house, nicely furnished, with the notable exception of the bed, which had a mattress that looked as if it had been the scene of a horrifically bloody crime in a brothel. We turned it over and concluded that there had been at least two crimes committed on it.

"Do you think six sheets are enough?" Sylvia wondered. She had divested a Chinese shop of its stock of sheets, and if one looked closely, one could see the overlapping contours of a Buddhist temple, a wooden bridge spanning a waterfall, a panda grazing on bamboo shoots, a pagoda, and a strutting peacock, a jumble of Chinese shadows.

Once moved in, we soon settled into our routines. Sylvia managed a few development projects for FSPI, which now and then took her far and wide around the region. Whereas in Kiribati she had dealt with excrement and disease, now she found herself involved with coral-reef restoration and promoting good governance. I worked at my book, and when I managed to reach my daily word count, I'd catch a minibus into town and spend the late afternoon walking around, idly wondering when I might feel at home here. Typically, whenever I move someplace new, which I have often enough, it takes me no time at all before I feel as if I am somehow a part of the world around me. Even when I had no desire to be a part of that world, as periodically happened in Kiribati, the circumstances of place, the peculiarities of geography, ensured that, like it or not, this was home. Port Vila, however, simply felt strange to me, and with each passing week, the town felt odder still. I'd find myself at the Rossi Restaurant, next door to the lingerie shop, sipping an espresso, idly perusing a faded *Paris Match* or *Le Figaro*, listening to the perfumed Frenchwomen planning a dinner party and the men discussing Marseille's prospects in the French soccer league, and I'd think, okay, this is where the French people hang out. Now and then, I'd meet Sylvia for a drink after work at the Office Pub, where we'd watch with mouths agape as the other customers, middle-aged Australian men, downed their stubbies while watching the footy on the telly and hurled the most startlingly colorful invectives at the cowering barmaids, whom they referred to as "darkies." All right, we thought, it appears that Australia has rednecks too, and this is where they gather. Some weekends, we'd find ourselves at Le Meridien resort, at the far end of Erakor Lagoon, where we'd rent a catamaran and sail the length of the lagoon, about two miles, and just as we'd near Erakor Village, a community off the electricity grid, a powerboat would be sent for us. "Shall I tow you back?" asked the resort employee. "No, it's all right," I'd explain. "I can sail, and the wind is fine, won't even require any tacking." But he'd be politely insistent, and I'd politely decline the rope, not because I was rude, but because I was prideful, and we'd compromise and I'd tack, turn the boat around, let out the sail, and glide under escort away from the men fishing in their wooden outrigger canoes and back toward the French teenagers waterskiing behind speedboats until we were safely docked at the resort, a gilded enclave lavishly decorated with the artwork of Vila's most prominent local artist, a gay Russian émigré. At dinner parties hosted by those employed to do good in Vanuatu, namely aid officials from the United Nations and the Asian Development Bank, I'd be asked, as a former employee of the World Bank, for my opinions regarding Vanuatu's development. I had some, and I offered them, feeling very self-conscious not least because I had hardly met any Ni-Vanuatu, except, briefly, for the servants who were silkily moving on the periphery of the dining room, clearing dishes, filling glasses.

It was as if there was a virtual wall separating us from the real Vanuatu. We inhabited the same geography, but we might as well have been on different planets. I found it most peculiar. Working on my book on Kiribati, I recalled that even though we'd had more money than the I-Kiribati—or rather, Sylvia had more money—there was no such wall. It didn't matter if you were Bill Gates; everyone swam in the same shit on Tarawa. In Port Vila, however, one could find pâté and smoked salmon at the Au Bon Marché, the local supermarket, and in the restaurants, diners were encouraged to eat coconut crab, an endangered species. But that was solely for Westerners. The Ni-Vanuatu ate laplap, a gooey paste of manioc cooked in an earth oven, or boiled taro. Most Westerners lived on the hillsides overlooking Vila Harbor. Most Ni-Vanuatu lived on the other side of those hills in shanties built of pilfered wood and tin.

It certainly wasn't unpleasant living in Vila. Frankly, I am very fond of smoked salmon and pâté. But it was strange in a way that I hesitated to define. Partly, this was due to the cost of living. New York and Tokyo are expensive places to live. This is unremarkable. But Vanuatu is firmly in the third world of nations. By every measurement—health, literacy, the status of women—Vanuatu ranks even lower than Kiribati, which is a low bar indeed. Typically, the upside to living in a poor country is that it's cheap. But as we settled in Port Vila, I was left utterly stupefied by the prices paid for basic utilities. Though we were very pleased that, unlike in Kiribati, these utilities were at least available in Port Vila, we found ourselves gasping whenever we received a bill. We had a refrigerator and a wall-unit air conditioner that we used only sporadically, and yet our monthly electricity bill was far higher than what we'd paid in Washington, D.C. It was the same with the phone bill. Basic telephone and Internet service cost more than ten times what we'd paid in the U.S., largely because power and telecommunications contracts had been awarded to private French companies. These were monopolies, and anywhere else in the world, utility monopolies would be tightly regulated, but in Vanuatu they were permitted to charge what they pleased. Similarly, basic groceries cost a small fortune. Vanuatu may not have had an income tax, which works out very well if you have a significant income, but it did have a value-added tax, which is not so good if you don't have much of an income. Most Ni-Vanuatu do not have a significant income. The expatriates, however, did.

If there was one service that did provide good value, it was minibuses. Simply stand alongside a road, and just by subtly quivering a pinky, you will soon see a minibus make a dramatic U-turn, pitch itself on two wheels, career across two lanes of traffic, and shudder to a halt with an emphatic skid in the dirt to pick you up. For less than a dollar, the bus driver will take you anywhere in Vila or its environs, though not necessarily by the most efficient route.

The journey from point A to point B is an ever-shifting calculation that depends on where the other passengers are going. Very often I'd find myself on a meandering dirt track that carved its way through a squatter settlement of shanties, where we'd deposit a schoolchild and pick up a young woman who'd soon be let off in front of a luxurious hilltop home with a stone fence lined with broken glass and a sign that said NEVER MIND THE DOGS. BEWARE OF OWNER.

"Is it just me," I said to Sylvia one day, "or does this place seem really weird to you too, like it's forever 1900 around here?"

"It's creepy," she agreed. "Have you seen the Frenchwomen shopping with their servants?"

"And what's up with the dogs?"

Many of the expatriates had dogs. Though Port Vila, like elsewhere in the Pacific, had no shortage of island dogs, many of the Westerners had imported purebreds from overseas, including little yapping, quivering dogs brightly festooned with bows. If such a dog were ever to be allowed outside the gates of its owner's villa, no doubt it wouldn't survive the afternoon once the island dogs were through with it. But the decorative dogs were never allowed outside the grounds. Even the dog community was segregated in Port Vila.

When explorer Pedro Fernandez de Quirós first alighted on Vanuatu in 1606, he established a short-lived Spanish colony called Nueva Jerusalema, and seeing how Westerners lived in Vila today it wasn't hard to discern a certain continuity between the original Western settlement and contemporary Port Vila. Fernandez de Quirós, feeling very pleased with himself for discovering what he assumed was the fabled southern continent of Australia, saw fit to appoint his ship's crew to rather exalted positions. "It was a marvelous thing to see such a diversity of knights," wrote a priest at the time, "for truly nothing like it has been seen since the world began, because there were sailor-knights, grummet-knights, ships' page-knights, mulatto-knights and Indian knights and knights who were just knight-knights." For the tax evaders and offshore bankers who now called Vanuatu home, Port Vila remained a Nueva Jerusalema, a place where they felt free to carry on like grummet-knights.

The most mystifying part, of course, was the reaction of the Ni-Vanuatu themselves. In America, if we were to allow a very small segment of the population to create an economic system that works entirely to their benefit while the vast majority of Americans simply scrape by, why we'd . . . call them shrewd businessmen and patriots and elect them to higher office. But if they were foreigners, why we'd . . . welcome them as investors. Perhaps, then, my feelings were misplaced. Perhaps there was nothing unnatural in the way society seemed to be organized in Port Vila, though it did seem uncomfortably colonial to me. The French were the functionaries, the Anglos the capitalists, the Chinese the shopkeepers, and the Ni-Vanuatu the hired help, admitted when necessary but otherwise kept outside the gates. Then, one morning, as I walked along the dirt road that led from our house toward the main road, I was greeted with a word that left me reeling in bewilderment.

"Gudmorning," I said in Bislama to the elderly man I encountered. He was shoeless, and he carried a bush knife. He regarded me with a friendly eye.

"Gudmorning, maste," he said.

Master. No, I thought. This is a very weird place.

CHAPTER 4

In which the author is introduced to kava, which he likes very much,
oh yes, very much indeed.

ONE OF THE GREAT BENEFITS OF LIVING ABROAD IS DIS-
covering that there's a whole new world of intoxicants to
explore. And I like intoxicants. Fortunately, I realized early on that I
had a predilection for chemically altering my state of mind, and so
by the time my friends were snorting their paychecks up through
their noses, I knew myself well enough to realize that, were I to do
even one line of cocaine, I'd soon find myself on the street turning
tricks for crack. Likewise with heroin. When a Bosnian acquaintance of mine in Prague suggested we shoot heroin together, I had
enough self-awareness to realize that, were I to join him, I'd have to
write off the next ten years of my life as I devoted myself to traveling the Needle Park circuit of Europe. Instead, I spent nearly ten
years trying to quit smoking, and painful and unpleasant as each of
those forty-three attempts were, I realized that it could be much,
much worse.

Still, even though I drew my line at hard drugs, there remained
a plethora of narcotics to enjoy, and I availed myself of all that came
my way. I like to think that I failed Algebra II in high school not because of any particular ineptitude with mathematics, but simply because of a quirk in my schedule. Algebra came after lunch, and the
lunch break, of course, was an excellent time to meander over into

the woods behind school, where everyday the potheads gathered to get baked. Xs and Ys were a buzz kill, so during the lesson, as I surreptitiously consumed my corn chips, I'd retreat to my own world, quietly giggling at the silliness of it all. During my senior year of college, I lived in an apartment in the Back Bay neighborhood of Boston, and at noon every day, when my three roommates and I woke up, the streets would become redolent with the sweet smell of cannabis as the bongs were lit for a morning pick-me-up. Wondering how else we could enliven our day, we soon discovered magic mushrooms, which we'd consume on our third-floor fire escape, and as the sunset played havoc with our sense of time and space and the people below began to resemble mutant anteaters, we'd have profoundly philosophical discussion on the nature of reality, questioning why was it that I saw anteaters whereas they saw turtles.

By the time I turned thirty, however, I had lost touch with the people who used to call to enquire whether I'd like to drop some acid with them and maybe spend an afternoon at the planetarium, or possibly just hang out at their mom's house and maybe watch *The Wall*—again. I wondered what had become of them, until I realized that they could probably still be found at their mom's house. Smoking weed with any kind of regularity also seemed like a rather juvenile thing to do, and after I made the near fatal mistake of wandering into a hash bar in Amsterdam, where I told the pot dealer to just give me the strongest stuff he had, I was cured of any desire to ever smoke weed again. There is stoned and there is comatose, and when finally, toward dawn, I was able to pry myself upright, I stumbled into the wreckage of the red-light district during the misty hour when the prostitutes and the addicts have had their fill and all that remains is waste and regret. Seeking to fortify myself, I bought a bag of *frites* and soon found myself greeting the new day on my knees, heaving my excesses into the gutter.

That was some time ago, and while I have found much to enjoy in wine, I remained amenable to finding other ways to tweak my experience with the world at large. In the U.S., exploring different ways to get stoned is a cumbersome and difficult thing to do. It is generally illegal, and this lends the enterprise a furtive, desperate sort of air. It is also dangerous. I am wary of consuming a concoction of chemicals "cooked" by an emaciated user with profusely bleeding gums. That's a red flag for me. Indeed, just about anything that involves cough syrup or complex formulas of chemical mixtures holds no interest for me. What I desired was the organic high. I think a little peyote in the desert might have worked, perhaps with the Navajo in New Mexico, around dusk, followed by some inspired drumming and chanting, but alas, the opportunity never presented itself.

Fortunately, I was now in Vanuatu, where getting profoundly stoned every night is a venerable tradition. In the golden hour before sunset, the men of Vanuatu gather in a *nakamal,* typically a clearing under a banyan tree, where they consume kava, which, to the uninitiated, is the most wretchedly foul-tasting beverage ever concocted by Man. Kava derives from *Piper methysticum,* a pepper shrub that thrives high in the hills of Vanuatu. Traditionally, the kava is prepared by having prepubescent boys chew the root until it becomes a mush of pulp and saliva, whereupon it is squeezed through coconut fiber, mixed with water, and swallowed all in one go from a coconut shell. Pondering this, you have to wonder *And whose idea was that?* I could not think of any circumstance where it would occur to me that consuming some kid's globby spitball might enhance my well-being. But we humans are a mysterious species, willing to try anything for a buzz, and fortunately for us, a long time ago, somewhere in Vanuatu, an enterprising individual discovered the secret to the most satisfying narcotic available for our pleasure.

That I would become such a connoisseur of kava, however, was not a forgone conclusion. I had tried it for the first time in Tonga, where, in strange circumstances, I attended a kava ceremony for a visiting Fijian princess. I had made a friend in Nuku'alofa, a Nepalese Sherpa—it's a long, digressive story—and we sort of invited ourselves and made ourselves comfortable sitting on the floor next to the princess, whom we knew only dimly. She was being honored by the Fijians living in Tonga, and unaware then what a big deal a kava ceremony was among Fijians and their aristocracy, we proceeded to make silly fools of ourselves. After a few bowls of kava, I turned to the princess, meaning to ask her how much kava, did she think, was too much kava. Instead, not yet realizing that kava's effect upon the mouth is similar to that of a shot of Novocain, I said: "Wincess, how wuch wava is woo wuch wava?"

My Nepalese friend thought this was hilarious. "You walk wunny," he said.

"You walk wunny woo," I pointed out, as we tumbled over in sidesplitting laughter.

We cracked each other up.

The effects soon wore off, however, and we were left with queasy stomachs and a growing awareness that we were making a faux pas of a nature that had escaped us. Kava, it seemed to me, was nothing more than a mild euphoric. It had made me a little tongue-tied, a little giddy, and I didn't understand what the Fijians were so serious about. All things being equal, I thought I'd much rather have a couple of beers.

This having been my only experience with kava, I entered the world of Vanuatu kava with an unfortunate disrespect for its power. We were invited one day to visit one of Port Vila's innumerable nakamals by Patricia, an American who worked with Sylvia, and her partner, Dirk, a Dutchman who worked as a handyman. On the outer islands, a nakamal was sacrosanct. In

Port Vila, a nakamal was simply a kava bar. At the time, Sylvia's organization was top-heavy with expatriates, and thus our early forays into our new milieu tended to be guided by foreigners. My work certainly didn't lend itself to the rapid acquisition of new friends. Writing, of course, is the most solitary of endeavors. You simply sit inside your own head for a while—and what a strange place that can be—and hopefully, after four or five hours, you have seven hundred words to show for it and you call it a good day. Now and then you find yourself wishing you had a co-worker, someone to complain with, just for form's sake, about the incompetent boss and the appalling work conditions, and you realize it's time to get out more. I was, therefore, looking forward to an evening at the nakamal, to be followed by a splendid meal at one of Port Vila's fine restaurants. I caught a minibus to Sylvia's office, a modest house on a hill behind the town center, where we soon found ourselves piling into Dirk's small compact. He drove us farther into the hills, and we spent the time talking about his last trip to Holland. I was born in Holland, and we reminisced about our mother country—how gray it was, how cold, how crowded, how soul-crushingly depressing winter could be, and how, despite these formidable strikes against the country, we both missed it enormously.

"It's the pubs that I really miss," Dirk said. "No one knows how to do a pub like the Dutch do. Even in the godforsaken villages of northern Friesland, you will still find a great pub."

I was in emphatic agreement. There is not a finer place to drink than in a cozy Dutch pub. On many a winter's eve—and there is not a crueler winter than those experienced in Northern Europe—when the wind and the bleak melancholic darkness left me trembling in despair, I only had to step inside a pub, almost any pub in Holland would do, where I would soon feel revived, not solely by alcohol—the Dutch have an unfortunate tradition of pouring their beer into pitifully meager glasses—but by a convivial atmosphere that I have not seen replicated anywhere else. And if that didn't work, there was always the hash bar next door.

We spoke for a while longer about what a fine country Holland was, until Sylvia asked whether he envisioned returning for good one day.

"Never," Dirk replied. "There is no kava in Holland. And there is no kava in the U.S., so I won't go there either."

Patricia rolled her eyes and sighed. Possibly an issue here, I thought. It was a curious reason for not going to Holland, of course. Never before had I heard anyone decry the lack of good narcotics as a reason for avoiding the Netherlands.

Dirk parked the car on the side of a dirt road, and we followed a narrow path to a clearing on a ridge overlooking the harbor. There was a breathtaking view of Iririki Island, surrounded by sailboats and the resort's catamarans. Farther on lay Ifira Island, home of the landowners who owned most of Port Vila, and even from a distance, the island exuded a prosperity not typically found on offshore islands in Vanuatu.

"What a stunning view," I said.

"It's even better after a few shells of kava," Dirk added.

In traditional Ni-Vanuatu culture, the nakamal is sacred ground. It is where inspiration is found for elaborate dances and rituals. It is where a man goes to speak with an ancestor or two. It is not a place for women. Until fairly recently, on many islands, if a woman stumbled into a nakamal, she would be punished by death. This is because women are impure. On this point, most cultures agree. From Eve onward, women have always been designated the impure ones. I've always found this curious. Compared to what? Nero? Attila the Hun? Dick Cheney? Me? They must be very impure indeed. Even more tragically, from a traditional Ni-Vanuatu point of view, the kava too would have to be discarded, and the men would have to wait a long time, upwards of twenty minutes, for the boys to chew and masticate another batch of kava roots. Things have changed, of course. Women are no longer killed for sullying the nakamal with their presence, though very often the kava would still be tossed.

In Port Vila, however, which is not at all like the rest of Vanuatu, no one even pretends that the nakamal is somehow holy ground. They are simply kava bars, and many will happily serve women, particularly foreign women, who are not bound by island tradition. The nakamal that Dirk had selected consisted of a corrugated tin shed and a couple of dusty wooden benches standing on a ridge overlooking the harbor. A half-dozen Ni-Vanuatu men sat there contentedly, now and then emitting a murmur or a great hork of phlegm.

"So what will it be?" Dirk asked. "Low tide or high tide?"

"Whatever you're having," I said confidently. I like to think that, when it comes to intoxicants, I can hold my own with just about anyone. Now and then, of course, this assumption has proven to be false, and I find myself keeled over, begging for mercy, as men with names like Ivan and Vladimir insist on just one more toast. But this was kava. Everyone in the South Pacific drinks kava, I figured, and based on my experience with it in Tonga, I saw no reason to be wary. Dirk asked the proprietor of the shed for two half-shells for the women and two full shells for us manly men. On the outer islands, a shell would be a coconut shell. But here in sophisticated Port Vila, our kava was served up in a glass cereal bowl. The proprietor dipped the bowls into a plastic bucket brimming with kava, and we brought them back to where Sylvia and Patricia stood.

"It doesn't look very appetizing," Sylvia said. "It looks like muddy water."

"Wait till you taste it," Patricia added. "You'll wish it was muddy water."

Clearly, this was different from drinking wine. With kava, one didn't admire its lush hue, or revel in its aromatic bouquet, or note the complex interplay of oak and black currant. This was more like heroin. Its consumption was something that was to be endured. The effect was everything. What concerned me, however, was not the taste but the possibility that this bowl of swirling brown liquid may have had as one of its essential ingredients the spit of unseen boys, which, frankly, I found a little off-putting.

"That's the best way to prepare kava," Dirk said. "It's very strong that way. There is something about chewing the root that really releases its strength. But here they simply grind the root to a pulp, and then they squeeze it through a sock and mix it with water."

A sock. I was beginning to realize that kava is like the sausage of the Pacific. One didn't really want to know how it was made.

I watched the Ni-Vanuatu men imbibe their shells and was struck by how different the culture of kava was here compared with elsewhere in the South Pacific. Kava is found on most of the islands of Melanesia and Polynesia. It is typically consumed communally, with men gathered around a large bowl, and a host passing a single shell among his guests. No formal event in Fiji or Tonga occurs without kava. But mostly, kava is used as a social lubricant. It is not uncommon for men in Fiji to spend an entire day around the kava bowl, shooting the shit, as it were, as they consume upwards of thirty shells. It's different in Vanuatu. No one drinks kava during the day. Not even the kavaheads, the true addicts. It is taken only around dusk and into the early hours of the evening. And more interestingly, I thought as I watched a man take his shell and wander away from his companions, one drinks kava alone in Vanuatu.

"What you do is this," Dirk said. "You take your bowl and find something nice to look at—the sunset, the stars, the trees—something poetic. Then, with that image in your mind, you take the kava all at once."

"And then what?" I asked.

"Then you listen to the kava."

"And try not to throw up," Patricia added.

So instructed, we each found a space of our own. It was not hard to find something poetic to admire. The sky was streaked with crimson, and a fresh breeze stirred the banana trees. The sailboats in the harbor bobbed in an alluring manner, and looking down from afar, I understood the appeal of just lingering here, in Port Vila, far from the continental world. A sailor had once explained to me that crossing the Pacific was the psychological equivalent of going to war: days and days of unrelenting tedium punctuated by moments of sheer, horrifying terror. Many had planned to circumnavigate the world, but after their experience in the Pacific—and from the Panama Canal to Vanuatu is a very long way, a journey that takes some boats two months to complete—some sailors found their ambitions deflated and chose, instead, to remain where they were, floating on their boats, savoring the splendor of sunset from the enchanting confines of Vila Harbor, lending their boats to the exotic, tranquil vista that I now stood contemplating, kava shell in hand. I closed my eyes, retaining the image in my mind, and brought my bowl to my lips. The odor was earthy and peppery, almost toxic, a bitter brew, and to send it down my gullet seemed unnatural, as if defying a hard-gained evolutionary warning trigger, the one that says that this is surely poison. I managed to swallow half the bowl before my stomach protested. I paused for a moment, asked my gut to refrain from sending the kava back up, because that would be really embarrassing, and when my stomach complied, I finished the remaining kava, emitting a groaning, squinting, incoherent curse, as a child might when forced to swallow acrid medicine. I returned my bowl to the kava shed, dimly noticing that it was taken and rinsed in a bucket of murky water, then stacked with the other bowls, awaiting the next user. Had I refreshed my hepatitis shots? I wondered. I couldn't remember.

"That was absolutely vile," I said a few moments later.

"Awful," Sylvia agreed.

"Here," Patricia offered. "Have some gum."

"Good kava today," Dirk said. "Very smooth. I find that, after a bowl of kava, a cigarette goes very well. Want one?"

I took the proffered Rothman's and, noting Sylvia's sidelong glance, immediately felt a solidarity with Dirk as we tended to the demands of our addictions. We spoke idly of work and the mysteries of Vanuatu, and it wasn't long before I felt suffused with a pleasant calmness, a contentment with my world. I wasn't certain whether this was attributable to the kava or to the inarguable fact that I was in a pleasant place, in the company of pleasant people, and that I was on the whole rather pleased with my world, sober or stoned. A blue twilight had overtaken the last embers of sunset, and the first stars of the evening appeared above Iririki Island. More men had arrived at the nakamal, and I half-expected to hear a hearty clamor, like that found in a bar after work, the happy foolery and repressed griping of people finally released from their obligations. But instead the din became ever more muted as the kava did its work.

"Another shell?" Dirk asked.

"I think so," I said.

Patricia declined another, but Sylvia, the trooper, was up for another half shell. It was my turn to pay, about two dollars for a half-shell and two full shells—considerably less than the cost of a single beer in one of the bars that lined Father Lini Highway, to say nothing of the cost of a beer in one of the resorts. I could carry only two bowls at a time; returning for mine, I was met by a Ni-Vanuatu man who was, like everyone else, clad in shorts and flip-flops.

"Hello," he said. "Where you from?"

"I've just arrived from America," I said.

"Ah," he said. "My name is Sam. I thought you from Australia. Not many people from America come to Vanuatu. Only Peace Corps. Are you Peace Corps?"

I admitted that I was not.

"Tourist? Not many tourists come to the nakamal."

I explained that I wasn't a tourist either, and that I was here, in his land, because my wife had a job here and I had followed her. "That's what I do," I explained. "I follow my wife around."

He thought this was very funny. "How many shells you have?"

"This will be my second."

"Two full shells already?" He emitted a low whistle. "Maybe you will have two-day kava."

"What's two-day kava?" I asked.

"That's when the kava talks to you for two days."

"Like a hangover?"

"No," he said. "Not like a hangover. Like a dream that doesn't end."

"But in Fiji," I noted, "people can drink thirty shells a day and still be alert in the morning."

"But this isn't Fiji kava. This is Vanuatu kava, from Pentecost Island. It is the best in the world. Very strong."

I asked him what his home island was.

"I am from Pentecost Island," he said.

Of course, I thought. Kava grows on every island with a hill in the South Pacific, and in conversations with other islanders, I had yet to meet anyone who didn't champion the supremacy of their own island's kava. In a nation a little more than twenty years old, an islander's primary loyalty was always to his home island. We each took our shell and sought a moment of poetry. The kava did not go down any easier this time. I still found it wretched, but I endured the bitterness because I think it's important to experience other cultures. And if it would get me stoned too, so much the better.

Soon we all found ourselves seated on a bench, chatting companionably with the nakamal's other patrons. Or, rather, Sylvia and Patricia were chatting with the nakamal's latest patrons. Those of us who had had more than a couple of shells had become strangely mute, as if lost in some distant reverie. I was happy to note that I wasn't the only one who had lost the urge to speak. This wasn't from any lack of sociability on my part. Indeed, I was beginning to feel as one with all.

Sam was seated next to me on the bench. He turned to me and said apropos of nothing: "America."

It wasn't a question, just a word, an image, an idea, and it hovered between us for a long moment, enveloping us. We silently communed about this thing called America. "Yes," I said finally, after we had exhausted the topic. There was nothing left to say, and we sat there happily, in a shared dream, feeling the slow drift of twinkling stars moving across the sky, until a thought occurred to me, which I shared with Sam.

"Vanuatu," I said.

Sam inhaled deeply. "Hmmm," he said. We pondered this for a long age, the nuances of Vanuatu, its essence, its magic. We breathed the scent of the islands, the thick tropical air, the sea, the vegetation, blooming flowers and rotting fronds. I stirred my flip-flops around in the dirt. A plume of dust. The dust of ages. Yes, the dust of ages. "Yes," said Sam at last, satisfied.

I was beginning to feel a bond with Sam. He was my brother. "Sam," I said. "Would you like another shell?"

He would.

I felt heavy. My steps were ponderous. "Are you all right?" I heard Sylvia ask. My wife. I felt the years together, the history, us. I loved her. "Splendid," I said, aglow, and I shuffled on with Sam to the shed.

"Tank yu tumas," Sam said.

"No, Sam. Tank yu tumas,"

Bislama, I thought. The language of poets. I took the bowl, a full shell. There was a light on the horizon, a flickering white orb. It was moving away from me. No. Toward me. I stared at the light. Come here, light. I drank the kava. I felt suffused with light.

I sat on the bench next to Sam, my brother. Smoked a cigarette. So sweet, this tobacco. Very heavy to lift this cigarette. I am, I thought. I am. Here. There are others. Such good people. They are my brothers. There is no time, no such thing. There is now, and it goes forever, on and on. Backward too, to the past. So heavy, this cigarette.

"Another shell?"

A voice. Whose voice? Dirk's. A good man, Dirk. He is my brother. "Yes," I said. Let us fly on.

Cannot move feet. Why do you not move, feet? Will speak to legs. Legs need help too. Push up with arms. Yes, standing now. Must get from here to there. Legs not moving. Why will you not move, legs? Ah, happy now. No need to move legs. Here is Dirk. A good man, Dirk. "Tank yu tumas." Difficult to speak. Shall stop speaking. Here is the kava. There are the lights, stars, my brothers. Good kava. Very smooth. Can sit down now.

Have missed bench.

Here is the dirt. Shall rest here. Dirty, this dirt is. Ashes to ashes, dust to dust. I am one with the dirt.

Who is this lifting me? Why, there is Sam. Hello, Sam. Can you hear me? Yes, you can. We are brothers. Thank you, Sam. There is my wife. Love her so. Shall tell her when mouth works. She is speaking. Go, she says. No, no, cannot go. Cannot move legs. Stay we must.

There is the moon. I see you, moon. Beautiful moon. I am watching you. Do you see me? I am one with you.

Still feel very heavy, so heavy. Shall sleep now.

Who is this carrying me? Hello, Sam. Hello, Dirk. My brothers. Do not carry me. Just let me lie here. I will be one with the dirt.

World is moving much too fast. Lights. Darkness. Lights again. Many more lights. Am inside a car. Do not like cars.

Here is my wife. Here is my house. No, no. Do not turn on lights. Lights must go off. Yes. The bed. Good idea. Shall just lie here for a moment. Am dreaming. Very strange dreams. Would like to wake up now. Cannot wake up.

IT WAS TWO DAYS before I returned to Earth, and many more before I ventured to another nakamal. I felt like I had been mugged, taken unawares, slugged from behind, and now I was wary. It had been a slow descent, nothing at all like a hangover, just a lingering sense that I was in a place far, far away, in a world of my own. "I asked the people at work," Sylvia said. "And they said you had way too much kava. You should have stopped at two shells."

"Well, maybe they should put a warning label on their kava."

Not that it would have made any difference. I had had five shells. There is nothing quite like knowledge gained through hard experience. No one expects his local drug dealer to affix labels on dime bags: WARNING. SMOKING DOPE WILL GET YOU STONED. It was all about balance, calibrating the intake of a narcotic so that it produced a desired sensation. But what I had achieved—gross inebriation, semiparalysis, hallucinations—was, from a traditional Ni-Vanuatu point of view, a desired outcome. Vanuatu is a world of rituals, magic, and sorcery. There are spirits and ghosts. Dead ancestors aren't quite as dead as they are in the West, and from time to time they drop by for a visit. The artwork of Vanuatu—headdresses adorned with the plumes of hawks, carved tree ferns, decorative tam-tams, or wooden drums—was, to my eyes, evocative and otherworldly. But in traditional Vanuatu they are not at all otherworldly. There is no distinction between the temporal and the spiritual, the physical and the metaphysical. This seems odd to the Westerner, accustomed as we are to the rigid distinction between the spiritual and the material. But in the West, we don't have kava. Drink enough kava and you too will hear voices in the wind. For this reason, in most villages in Vanuatu, kava was not a daily libation. It was reserved for ceremonies and rituals, and it is then, when you are good and stoned, that you might hear dear departed Uncle Al speak to you from the beyond, encouraging you to dance like a cosmic rooster.

In Port Vila, I was learning, kava was something else entirely. There were hundreds of nakamals scattered throughout town. If one wanted to chat with the minister of agriculture or any other high-level government official, there was a very good likelihood of finding him at Ronnie's nakamal, near the parliament. This was a favorite nakamal for expatriates, but as time went by, I came to prefer my local nakamal. Our neighborhood was typical in its peculiarity. On one side of a gutted dirt road, the side that offered a view, stood the lavish homes of Westerners, spacious villas that hummed with air conditioners, nestled behind high walls and electronic gates, guarded by rottweilers and German shepherds. On the other side of the road were the modest bungalows of Port Vila's civil servants, each containing an extended family, perhaps even two extended families. Interspersed throughout the hilltop were the dwellings of land squatters, shanties built of wood and tin. Our immediate neighbors were land squatters from Tanna Island, and like so many other compounds on our road, in the evening their home became a nakamal. It was really quite extraordinary. During the day, their land was alive with women and children, friendly, energetic little people with the coolest hair ever. They were like Rasta munchkins, sprouting frizzled blond manes. I had thought that blond hair was limited to those of European stock, but it wasn't at all unusual to see children with blond plumes in Vanuatu, though not adults. In the evening, however, they were nowhere to be seen as their home was transformed into a nakamal, one of a half dozen that appeared in our small neighborhood. Each evening toward sunset, hundreds of red lanterns were turned on in front of the nakamals throughout Port Vila, signaling that the kava had been prepared and they were open for business.

"I think I'll go meet the neighbors," I said to Sylvia one evening after I noticed the beckoning red light.

Sylvia looked at me dubiously. "Moderation, okay? I can't carry you by myself."

I had little inclination to leave the planet again—well, perhaps into a low Earth orbit—so when I appeared inside the neighbor's shed, I asked for a sensible half-shell of kava. Stepping outside, I had a view of our house just down the hill and, beyond, the green eminences sheltering Mele Bay. I noticed that the fruit in our papaya tree was about to ripen and that it wouldn't be long until we'd have another bushel of bananas to gorge on. A lush country, I thought. I sought my moment of poetry and downed the kava, which once again tasted dreadfully toxic.

"Me likem kava," I said congenially to the bucket ladler as I returned my shell.

"Kava blong Tanna," he said. And then I became lost as he spoke in Bislama at a clip far too fast for me to comprehend.

"Me no save tok-tok Bislama quicktime," I said. "Yu tok-tok slow-time, me save."

Well, some of it in any case. Bislama's unique fusion of English, French, and indigenous words had a rhythm and logic that I found very appealing. The word for "pope," for instance, was *numba wan jesus man*. But when spoken rapidly, and to my ears it was always spoken rapidly, Bislama was like gibberish, vaguely familiar but unintelligible.

Inside the kava shed, we spoke some more in Bislama—he spoke neither English nor French—and I was led to understand that the kava from Tanna was the strongest in Vanuatu. It may very well be. I certainly wasn't going to test the proposition, and this time I thought it prudent to wait a while before imbibing another shell. I took my place on a bench outside and chatted in the halting manner of someone unsure of whether he was making any sense. The other patrons, who were in various states of kava-induced bliss, were all from Tanna, an island known for cargo cults, kastom people, and for possessing the world's most accessible live volcano. In Port Vila, fairly or unfairly, the people of Tanna had acquired a reputation as troublemakers. Indeed, just a few weeks prior, one of the regulars at the Office Pub, an Australian banker, had been brutally killed as he left the bar. The murderers were from Tanna. Much more typical, however, were break-ins, which is why a good many of the Westerners in Vila had turned their homes into fortresses.

"Yu likem kava?" asked one of my companions on the bench. He appeared to be a little younger than I was and wore a beard and a T-shirt emblazoned with a rapturous Bob Marley.

"Me likem kava blong Tanna," I said. This was clearly a very satisfactory answer, and the others nodded agreeably.

"Yu likem Vanuatu?" I was asked.

"Me likem Ni-Vanuatu tumas. Me ting Vanuatu bugger-up."

My companions nodded sagely. I was, apparently, entirely of

their way of thinking. The people were very good, they agreed. The country, however, was bugger-up.

"Yu wanem wan shell kava?" I asked, suddenly feeling very expansive. Evidently, we were all on the same wavelength here, and as evening gave way to darkness and the only lights to be seen came from a kerosene lantern hanging in the kava shed and from those of my own house, I began to hear the kava. These are my people, I thought. True, we may be of different races. And our cultures might be wildly at odds with each other. And my shirt might not be as riddled with holes as theirs. But we are brothers.

"Yu blong wea?" I was asked.

Say what?

"Yu stap wea?"

Seeing my bafflement, he made as if to sleep. "Wea?" Where?

"Ah . . . mi blong . . ." I couldn't find the words, and so I pointed at my house. "Mi blong there."

This was duly noted.

"Yu gat woman?"

Indeed I did, which reminded me that I had promised to return home while I still possessed my dignity and, ideally, my mobility.

"And?" Sylvia asked, as I stumbled in, immediately dimming the lights.

"I'm as sober as a judge," I assured her, and then I spent the next hour admiring the faint play of moonlight dancing on a palm frond.

Sylvia didn't much care for kava. She found the taste repellent, which it inarguably was, and after we had been in Vila long enough, she had come to recognize the kavaheads and the fact that there were an awful lot of them, including a good proportion of Vila's expatriate men. Kava acts as an appetite suppressant. Ideally, for kava to do its wonders, one shouldn't eat for three or four hours prior to imbibing. After a kava session, there is no desire for food, except

possibly, for a slice of papaya or a banana. Heavy kava users are invariably rail thin. Indeed, the Frenchwomen in Vila were known to use kava as a diet drug. Now and then, because social life in Vila revolves around the nakamals, Sylvia would join me for a shell at Ronnie's, and having recently come from America, where a goodly percentage of citizens tend toward the rotund, it was rather remarkable to see such a gathering of skinny Westerners. But that was the extent of her forays. "I feel like the designated driver," she said. I, however, was discovering that I was immensely fond of kava, and two or three times a week I'd find myself eagerly awaiting the lighting of the red lanterns.

At the neighbor's nakamal, I'd have languorous discussions with the other patrons about the issues of the day. They were necessarily languorous, of course, because as the evening wore on it became increasingly challenging to attach words to ideas. Nevertheless, I came to greatly enjoy these conversations. I felt my presence at the neighborhood nakamal was what allowed us to live in an unsecured house, lacking gates or bars on the windows, without fear of a break-in. "They even took my bed," said a friend, a Canadian volunteer, who had been robbed. "It was a king-size bed too."

"Do you patronize your local nakamals?" I asked.

"No," he said. "I go to Ronnie's."

Subsequently, he did visit his local nakamal, where he had kava with the neighborhood chief, who arranged to have his belongings returned to him, bed included.

ONE EVENING the talk in the nakamal turned to Mir, the Russian space station, which was expected to crash on Vanuatu the follow-

ing day. If it were to hit one of the islands, the government informed us, it would be like Hiroshima, a cataclysmic explosion, destroying all life on the island. Just as bad, the government confidently declared, would be a splash-down in Vanuatu's waters. All coastal villages were told to evacuate to higher ground. Enormous tsunamis were expected. The government prudently declared a state of emergency and abolished parliament. This had nothing to do, the government announced, with the no-confidence vote it had been expected to lose the next day.

"Yu whiteman," a fellow patron said, addressing me. "Wanem yu ting?" He wanted to know my thoughts about the impending catastrophe. There are not many subjects I am less qualified to expound upon than the scientific principles affecting a spacecraft reentering Earth's atmosphere, particularly when compelled to do so in a language that I only dimly understood. Nevertheless, assisted by another shell of kava, which allowed me to see the big picture, I used a stick to draw the Earth, encircled it with another ring, which I called "air," and tried to explain that when a spacecraft hit the atmosphere at high speed, it burned up, and if anything managed to survive the inferno, it was likely to be small and inconsequential. "Vanuatu olraet. No Hiroshima. No tsunami."

What about the driver? someone asked.

"No driver."

So who's steering?

Well, this stumped me. Who was steering? How exactly does one guide a spaceship down? I felt fairly certain that it involved computers. But how typing a phrase or a code on a keyboard could possibly affect the course of an object hurtling through space was well beyond my understanding. It was the same with telephones. How exactly does one's voice travel thousands of miles, more or less instantaneously, without even passing through wires or cords? My brain began to throb. These were the wrong kinds of thoughts for kava. Finally, I offered the only answer that made sense to me: "Me ting magic."

My companions nodded thoughtfully. "Whiteman magic," one said.

I couldn't say. But after I had another shell of kava, I knew one thing. "Kava Vanuatu magic."

CHAPTER 5

In which the author is reduced to a state of wondrous awe as the prime minister of Vanuatu conspires to sell his country in exchange for a ruby, a giant ruby, which curiously no one is allowed to examine.

O SUGGEST THAT THE GOVERNMENT OF VANUATU WAS A trifle corrupt would be wrong. It was spectacularly corrupt. Indeed, I believe they even held seminars in corruption: Malfeasance 101, or How to Get Rich on a Government Wage. Whenever a new honorary consul was appointed, one knew something was afoot. The Vanuatu government was indignant, however, when Britain refused to accept its latest honorary consul, Dr. Peter Chen Hun-kee. Apparently, having served eighteen years in prison in Hong Kong for gold robbery was a disqualification for the London post.

It was the appointment, however, of Amarendra Nath Ghosh as the nation's Consul General, Roving Ambassador, and Trade Representative to the Kingdom of Thailand, Laos, and South Australia that soon had everyone atwitter. In gracious acknowledgment of the honor, Ghosh, who claimed to be a Thai citizen, donated a garbage truck to Vanuatu, and in case anyone was unsure where this shiny new garbage truck came from, he had it emblazoned with a sign that read DONATED BY A. N. GHOSH, CONSUL GENERAL AND ROVING AMBASSADOR. Touched by the gesture, the government waived the ten-year residency requirement and granted him citizenship. Soon, Vanuatu's latest Roving Ambassador was building a palatial home for himself on the hillside overlooking Erakor Lagoon, and he promised to build a luxurious walled compound for members of the cabinet. For good measure, he threw in a new international airport too, capable of handling 747s. Why not? Those who followed politics in Vanuatu were left wondering—what now?

Since independence, Vanuatu has been ruled by what in Melanesia are called Big Men, high-ranking men from powerful tribal clans. The first was Father Walter Lini, an Anglican minister who presided over Vanuatu for its first ten years as an independent nation. Things got off to a rough start, however, when a radical American libertarian organization called the Phoenix Foundation decided that Espíritu Santo, the largest island in Vanuatu, would make for an excellent libertarian utopia. It was to be called the Republic of Vemarana. The foundation funded and armed a secessionist group led by Jimmy Stephens, which soon declared the island's independence. As Vanuatu did not yet have an army, Lini was compelled to call in troops from Papua New Guinea to crush the rebellion. Father Lini, however, soon made himself popular by repatriating the land that prior generations of Ni-Vanuatu had sold or were coerced into giving to planters and colonists. Even today, foreigners cannot own land in Vanuatu, though they may lease it. Soon, however, Lini's government was as riddled with corruption, cronyism, and nepotism as any banana republic's, setting the stage for his successors. Since then Vanuatu, even by the impressive standards of Melanesia, has been notoriously unstable. Its Big Men plot and maneuver to topple any government not led by themselves. A government rarely lasts longer than a year or two before another Big Man succeeds in buying off a sufficient number of ministers of parliament to enforce a change.

Among Vanuatu's Big Men, one has long distinguished himself—
Barak Sope. He looked, in my opinion, remarkably like Idi Amin
with Don King's haircut, a shocking frizzle of gray that suggested he
had some personal experience with forks and power outlets. In parliament, Sope was the distinguished representative from Ifira Island,
across the bay from Port Vila. He became prime minister when his
uncle, Ati Sokomanu, who happened to be the president of Vanuatu
at the time, appointed him to the position. Apparently, this was illegal, and they both went to jail. One would think that attempting a
coup would be enough to end a political career, but people in Vanuatu are loyal to their own, and the people of Ifira Island reelected
Sope to parliament. Soon he was back in court, trying to explain
why exactly he was importing thousands of machine guns, mines,
and anti-tank weapons into the country from China. His correspon-
dence on the matter was written on the letterhead of the Central Intelligence Department. Vanuatu doesn't have a Central Intelligence
Department. Sope said that he was merely trying to "defend the sacred honor of the motherland."

Well, surely, you think, attempting to create a private militia to
challenge the country's security forces would be a career-ender. In
Vanuatu, however, this got him a job as minister of finance, and
here is where Barak Sope demonstrated his true genius. Say what
you will about Sope, but he has gumption. He began a lucrative
sideline selling Vanuatu passports, then moved on to issuing official
promissory notes worth tens of millions of dollars to an Australian
swindler. The financial collapse of the country was prevented only
by the intervention of Scotland Yard.

The national ombudsman of Vanuatu, a courageous French-
woman who had endured death threats, issued a public report stating that Barak Sope should never again be allowed to participate in
the governance of Vanuatu. Barak Sope then became prime minister.

Shortly after we arrived in Port Vila, Prime Minister Sope decided that Vanuatu's interests could best be advanced by allying itself closely with—of all the countries in the world—Laos. Vanuatu, Sope declared, would invest in Laotian agriculture and mining and help finance the country's infrastructure. For good measure, Vanuatu would also help Laos launch satellites into space. With what? I wondered. A slingshot? Clearly, the prime minister had had a few shells. I wasn't sure what the Laotian government thought of this sudden benevolence, though I did think it telling that the only agreement it signed was one pledging "non-interference in each other's internal affairs." Amarendra Ghosh was to be the first ambassador to Laos.

Barak was up to something, people said in the nakamals. *The Trading Post*, Port Vila's liveliest newspaper, began to investigate. The publisher was an Englishman who had lived in Vanuatu for a little more than a decade. His newspaper had a decidedly English orientation, and each day, somewhere in its pages, one could reliably find a picture of a buxom woman in a string bikini—*The Brazilian model Eva Jiggles enjoying the sun in Rio*. Much of the paper was devoted to the travails of the English soccer player David Beckham and his wife, Super Spicy, or was it Silly Spicy? The real appeal of the paper, however, was in its "Mi herem say" section. This translates as "I heard that . . . ," and this is where readers had an opportunity to share all the lascivious gossip they had acquired. I am not ashamed to admit that this was the section of the newspaper that got me on the road to learning Bislama. Here were lively tales involving besotted kavaheads and drunken ministers. Did you see the minister of agriculture getting hot and heavy with a bargirl? *The Trading Post* wanted to know. Imagine American newspapers reporting the salacious details involving, say, the president's daughter, and how she had been seen, severely inebriated, vomiting in the alley . . . okay, scratch that, let me think of another example. Imagine stumbling across your neighbor, Mrs. Smith, in flagrante with someone who very clearly was not Mr. Smith. Dying to tell someone? Well, *The Trading Post* is there for you. It's that good.

The rest of the paper, however, read like a compendium of press releases issued by the local foreign-aid industry. SAVE THE PIGS BEGINS DRIVE TO END CRUEL TREATMENT OF SWINE, or INSTITUTE FOR THE ADVANCEMENT OF POVERTY GIVES THREE COMPUTERS TO VILLAGE ON MALEKULA; ELECTRICITY TO FOLLOW. It was with some surprise, then, that all of a sudden, with four-inch headlines, the paper began to publish its investigation into the Sope government. One of its first articles reported the unsavory background of Sope's choice for honorary consul to Britain. One could imagine Sope thinking, *And what do the snoots in England have against gold robbery?* The paper then discovered that Amarendra Nath Ghosh might in fact not be a Thai citizen, and that he was being investigated in Singapore for fraud.

This made for compelling reading, and Sylvia and I looked forward to each new installment. The government, however, took a rather dim view of the investigation, and it wasn't long before the newspaper's lead story became TRADING POST PUBLISHER DEPORTED. Sometime before dawn, Vanuatu's security forces had arrived to arrest the publisher at his home.

I didn't envy him. We had had our own rather unfortunate experience with the security forces. On Christmas Day, as we were walking down toward Erakor Lagoon, where we had planned to go for a swim, Sylvia had been accosted. Christmas, alas, is the one time a year when a good deal of the men in Vila abandon kava in favor of hard liquor, with the result that, for the holiday season, Vila is the scene of considerable mayhem and the town's pleasant air gives way to one exuding malice. As we passed a group of men drinking, one besotted fool reached for Sylvia. Well, suffice it to say that things soon escalated, and we were on the cusp of coming to blows, when suddenly the bleary-eyed drunk pulled out a machete from his filthy backpack. His companions, all as drunk as he was, joined him. Several were carrying machetes. "Let's go," Sylvia urged. This, I thought, was an entirely unsatisfactory ending. I was fairly frothing with adrenaline, and it took a long moment before it dawned on me that if I didn't walk away, I would be dead momentarily.

Luckily, word of the encounter quickly reached the resort at the bottom of the hill. Passersby had assumed we were tourists from the resort and rushed to inform the staff, who called the security forces. Our little scene must have created quite the impression as a busload of tourists arrived just in time to see three pickup trucks packed with fatigues-clad soldiers pull up in front of the resort. They told us to come with them, and it wasn't long before they found the machete-wielding drunk. They threw him into the back of a truck and proceeded to beat him senseless, which, frankly, I had no quibble with.

The impression we took away was that Vanuatu's paramilitary police force were not the sort of people one wanted showing up at your home at five o'clock in the morning. The publisher was taken to the airport, deposited on an early morning flight to Australia, and soon found himself in Brisbane, where, no doubt, he could be heard muttering, "What just happened?" The government declared that The Trading Post had been publishing "state secrets" that were "detrimental to investors' confidence in Vanuatu." Most egregiously, the publisher had not respected Vanuatu's culture, and for this he was deported.

Fortunately for one and all, the deportation was deemed illegal by the country's chief justice, and the publisher returned to Vanuatu just in time for The Trading Post to announce that Mr. Ghosh had very kindly donated a giant ruby to the good people of Vanuatu. It was, he said, worth $175 million. Prime Minister Sope was delighted, and he announced that, using the ruby as collateral, the government of Vanuatu planned to issue $300 million in bonds. The recipient would be Amarendra Nath Ghosh, who promised—he may have even crossed his heart—to use some of the money to finance a paved road around Efate. Soon Ghosh was also given mineral, fishing, and forest concessions in Vanuatu, and even the right to issue currency in Vanuatu's name.

Well, this must be some ruby, everyone thought, and we were looking forward to seeing it. Alas, no one was ever allowed to see the enormous gem. It was hidden, for the common good, in a secret location somewhere in Port Vila. Fortunately, a picture of the ruby was soon released. It looked remarkably like a rock. Indeed, it was a rock, said a gem expert quoted by the newspaper. Nonsense, said the government. Ghosh had smuggled the gem out of Burma himself. Well, even if it was a gem, wasn't stealing it from Burma illegal? A trifling detail, replied the Sope administration.

What a curious state of affairs, we thought. I wondered how a nation could endure it. Of course, on the outer islands, where the vast majority of Vanuatu's population live, there was little inkling that anything was amiss. Still, I was curious as to what those in Port Vila, who did have access to the newspaper, thought about Barak Sope and the giant ruby. In the name of research, I decided to spend a little more time at the nakamals.

"Barak Sope is a great leader. All the world respects him," said one dapperly dressed man at Ronnie's nakamal. The others nodded encouragingly.

"But don't you think he's being just a tad reckless, giving Ghosh $300 million in exchange for a ruby that no one is allowed to see?"

"But you see," said my companion, a government official, "Barak knows everything there is to be known about money. Barak is a very smart man." Pause. "He is my uncle."

It occurred to me that I was in the wrong nakamal.

At the neighborhood nakamal, however, the mood was decidedly different. The kava drinkers were upset, angry even, that once again the Ifira Mafia—for that is how they viewed Port Vila's landowners—was robbing the country blind. For a brief moment, I wondered if Vanuatu might finally go the way of the rest of Melanesia: mayhem and anarchy in Papua New Guinea, civil war in the Solomon Islands, a coup in Fiji.

"Yu wanem wan shell kava?" asked my benchmate.

"Tank yu tumas," I said as we found our moments of poetry, and as I joined the kava drinkers on the bench for a quiet, relaxing, stress-free reverie, it occurred to me that no, nothing will happen in Vanuatu, not while we listened to the kava.

CHAPTER 6

In which the author ponders cannibalism and discovers that he just doesn't get it—not at all, cannot get past the icky factor—and so, left to his own devices by his beguiling wife, he decides to seek enlightenment on the island of Malekula, where until recently, within his own lifetime even, they lunched on people.

NOW AND THEN, I LIKE TO THINK THAT WE HUMANS ARE understandable, that for every conceivable action there is some reason driving it, some underlying cause or instinct that makes our behavior, if not logical, at least comprehensible. Lust, for instance. That's a big one. Where would we be without lust? I daresay we wouldn't be here at all. Hunger, power, a desire for security—primal, animalistic impulses—these too are all great motivators of behavior. Were one to listen to the grim reductionism offered by evolutionary biologists, one might conclude that all behavior is coldly guided, driven by a simple need to ensure that our genes continue on without us. That seems inadequate to me. Think of all the ways teenage boys, for example, conspire to take themselves out of the gene pool. They do this because, periodically, we are all stupid, and I am willing to acknowledge that simple, base stupidity can explain a lot of behavior. I speak with some experience.

Thinking on a grander scale—and why not fly those lofty airs?—one might ask why societies do what they do. What motivates them?

Why, for instance, does one culture send men to the moon (to play golf, of course), whereas another culture will worship it from afar, now and then quivering in terror during a lunar eclipse? This is the territory covered by Jared Diamond in *Guns, Germs, and Steel: The Fates of Human Societies,* a very satisfying book for people like me, who like to think there is a reason behind everything. Diamond argues, very persuasively, that society is shaped by its environment—that its direction is determined by soil fertility, the surrounding animal life, its relative isolation from other societies, even its continental axis—and that nothing changes a culture faster than a change in its environment. I found this very compelling and, finishing the book, I thought, *Well, there you have it. Humanity explained. Finally.* But then there is Vanuatu, which has many peculiar customs, and if there was one custom that defied my book learning, that confounded my understanding of human nature, it was cannibalism. What to make of it? What would compel someone to eat another person?

Most people are aware of instances of cannibalism that result from extreme deprivation. We are familiar with the Donner party and their unfortunate travails in the High Sierras. Hollywood has given us *Alive,* a dramatization of the events that befell a rugby team when their plane crashed in the remote Andes. Grisly as those events were, we can empathize with those who, having no other means to remain alive, take it upon themselves to eat the bodies of their dead companions. Remaining among the living, by any means necessary, is an instinct that is easily understood. No doubt cannibalism of this nature has occurred since we first became carnivores. But as I noted the banana trees and papaya trees that sprouted like weeds in our yard, and as I snorkeled among a million fish, I thought it unlikely that the cannibalism that prevailed throughout Vanuatu had anything to do with sustenance. Nor was it the case, as it was on some islands in Micronesia, that cannibalism in Vanuatu was a form of ancestor worship. In Kiribati, for instance, when someone dies, it is customary for family members to partake of the flesh of the decomposing corpse, ladling it into a kind of soup, which is then consumed, ensuring that, for those in bereavement for Grandma, she will always remain a part of them. I'd prefer a wake of a different sort, but as someone raised as a Catholic, I could get my head around the custom. That starchy wafer produced by nuns, given to us toward the end of Mass—provided, of course, that we had confessed our sins and performed our penance (four Hail Marys and three Our Fathers, typically, for not making up my bed, being mean to my sister, and having unholy thoughts)—was, we were assured by Father David, the very flesh of Jesus.

"But it's just a wafer," I had exclaimed during one of the question-and-answer sessions Father David held for us sprites each month at St. Bonaventure.

"It is the body of Christ," he assured me, and sensing some Protestant proclivities on my part, he went on and explained, once again, what the Holy Eucharist was about, a lesson that to this day remains a little fuzzy for me.

"But . . . it doesn't taste like a person. It tastes like a wafer."

Nevertheless, while I may not have completely understood what Holy Communion was all about, Catholicism did allow me to see the nuances in cannibalism. Eating the flesh of another human being, I understood, might not always be a really, really bad thing to do. If you were a good Catholic, you had some every Sunday. And, stretching my capacity for understanding human behavior about as far as it would go, I could see how eating the flesh of your dead family members might not be an appallingly deviant thing to do. But this was not how cannibalism was practiced in Vanuatu. Cannibalism there was more like the cannibalism practiced by Jeffrey Dahmer: very disturbing.

Until very recently, island life in Vanuatu had been character-

ized by a state of endless war. This is where my struggle to understand cannibalism begins, for no war seems more pointless to me
than the kind traditionally waged in Vanuatu. Typically, the men of
a particular village ambushed the men of another village. The goal
was to capture one man, who would then be triumphantly carried
back to the attackers' village, clubbed, and chopped into pieces.
Good manners dictated that an arm or a leg be sent off to a friendly
village. Again here, I sputter in disbelief. Imagine receiving such a
package. "Oh, look, honey. Bob and Erma over in Brooklyn have
sent us a thigh. So thoughtful." Of course, now you are obliged to
reciprocate, and so you gather your friends and off you go, hunting
for a man, and when you capture one, you will thoughtfully hack an
arm off and send it along to Bob and Erma, together with a note—
Thinking of you. Meanwhile, no village will tolerate the loss of a man
or two without seeking vengeance, and so off they go, looking for
you, and just as you're taking your leisure underneath your favorite
banyan tree, perhaps digesting a meal, you may find yourself surrounded by fierce-looking men wearing nothing more than leaves
around their penises and carrying heavy, knotted clubs, and suddenly you know that this day is not going to end well. You will be
carried, kicking and screaming, to the enemy's village, a village that
once contained men named Henry, Kenny, Luther, and Jeremiah,
but they're not there anymore, and you know why. You ate them.
And now it is your turn to be devoured. If you are very lucky, a good
solid blow to your head will the end the misery right there and then,
sparing you the sensation of feeling your body treated like a boiled
lobster as your flesh and bones are plucked and torn, carved and
diced, cooked in flames, until nothing remains of you except the
faint odor of a satisfied belch. But worry not. Bob will avenge you.

When Westerners began to arrive in some numbers in the nineteenth century, they too found themselves participating in Vanu-

atu's exciting culinary world. John Williams, the very first missionary to arrive in Vanuatu, landed on the island of Erromango on November 18, 1839. Sponsored by the London Missionary Society, which had had considerable success in converting much of Polynesia to Christianity, Williams stepped ashore, no doubt confident that very soon he would be breaking bread with the islanders. Within minutes, he was dead, killed by a fusillade of arrows. And then he became lunch. A half-dozen other missionaries would suffer the same fate, and it wasn't long before Erromango came to be known as the Island of Martyrs. In 1847, the *British Sovereign* had the great misfortune of finding itself wrecked off Efate. Twenty crew members escaped the sinking vessel on a small boat and made their way to shore, where they were happily received by the islanders. And who wouldn't be happy to see such a feast? In the end, only two of the unfortunate sailors managed to elude the dismal fate of their companions, who could last be heard asking their hosts, "You're having what for dinner?"

In the latter half of the nineteenth century, the blackbirders began to visit the islands of Vanuatu. Little better than slavers, they were recruiters searching for indentured workers to toil in the mines of New Caledonia and the sugar and cotton plantations of Fiji, Samoa, and Australia. Many Ni-Vanuatu were kidnapped. Most suffered through years of appalling brutality, but if they survived their years of service, they were returned to their islands. *Survived* being the operative word. Of the forty thousand Ni-Vanuatu lured to Queensland, Australia, fewer than thirty thousand lived to return. Of the ten thousand who were sent to New Caledonia, Fiji, and Samoa, it is unknown how many lived, though the mines in New Caledonia were known to be a graveyard. Some of those who did manage to return, quite naturally, held a grudge against white men.

In 1878, on the island of Ambae, a returned laborer named Sik-

eri was in need of victims. For men in Vanuatu, prestige and influence were obtained by passing through demanding grade-taking
rituals, which allowed a man to move upward in class. On most islands, a chief earned his position by participating in ceremonies
that called for an ever-greater sacrifice of pigs. Pigs equaled wealth
in Vanuatu. Now and then, however, a grade-taking ritual required
the sacrifice of men, and so when recruiters from the *Mystery* arrived one fine morning, Sikeri and his followers decided that they
would do nicely. Six men were slaughtered and eaten. Three years
later, a similar fate befell the crew of the *May Queen* when another
chief on Ambae needed victims to commemorate the death of his
child.

But why eat people? Killing people I could understand. It happens all the time. A quick glance at the local news suggests that
human beings kill one another for the most trivial of reasons. Indeed, I daresay I too have felt the urge to kill, particularly when I'm
driving. If the driver of the white Ford F-150 pickup truck that cut
me off last Tuesday is reading this, you should know that I'm looking for you. And in Vanuatu, when one considers what happened
subsequent to the arrival of Westerners, it is a wonder that the Ni-
Vanuatu did not kill every missionary, sandalwood trader, and
colonist who landed upon their shores. Perhaps no country suffered
more cruelly from the diseases introduced by Westerners than Vanuatu. Living in such isolation from the rest of the world, the Ni-
Vanuatu had not acquired immunity to influenza, measles, whooping
cough, and a half-dozen other ailments. What caused a sniffle in
London killed in Vanuatu. When the unfortunate Mr. Williams arrived on Erromango in 1839, there were approximately 4,500 people living on the island; by 1930, there were only 500. Aneityum
Island had a population of 3,500 in 1850; in 1905, there were 450.
On every island touched by Westerners, epidemics followed, and the

depopulation of Vanuatu was appalling. In 1800, an estimated one million Ni-Vanuatu lived on the islands. By 1935, there were only 41,000. "Why should we have any more children?" asked one woman on Malekula. "Since the white men came, they all die."

Local medicine and magic were no antidote to the apocalyptic waves of disease that swept through Vanuatu during the nineteenth and early twentieth centuries. On many islands, epidemics were understood to be the work of sorcerers who had the power to both cause and cure illness. This was a belief that did not work well for missionaries. The death of John Williams had hardly hindered their efforts to convert the Ni-Vanuatu, though the London Missionary Society did think it prudent to send Samoan missionaries for a while to soften the heathens up, as it were, rather than lose another Englishman. For those missionaries who did manage to establish a presence on an island, their work tending to those overcome by measles, smallpox, and the other epidemics of the day was regarded as evidence that they had caused the disease, and for this many were killed and eaten. Some missionaries even went out of their way to take responsibility for an epidemic. When measles swept through Erromango in 1861, George Gordon, an obstinate Presbyterian from Canada, declared that it was his god who did this—a little payback for their stubborn heathenism. Now that the mystery of who was to blame was all cleared up, the islanders felt free to carve up Gordon and his wife for dinner, a fate that befell innumerable missionaries during those dark years.

It is grim stuff. Perusing the country's history, one begins to realize that Vanuatu is like the Russia of the South Pacific, a place of endless calamities. Most of the misery that befell Vanuatu, alas, is hardly unique. To this day, as Rwanda and Yugoslavia demonstrate, we still find a reason to kill our neighbors. And the diseases that wiped out the Ni-Vanuatu were the same diseases that brought the indigenous peoples of the Americas to the cusp of extinction. A first encounter with someone from the Eurasian landmass was very often the equivalent of a death sentence for the rest of humanity, who had the misfortune of residing in places bereft of the cows and horses and other domesticated animals that conferred a measure of immunity. All this I understood. What continued to baffle me, however, was cannibalism. Not the occasional ceremonial cannibalism, not cannibalism as vengeance, not the *I really need to eat* kind of cannibalism. What perplexed me was the almost casual nature of cannibalism in Vanuatu, its everydayness. As far as I understood, there was neither shame nor reverence attached to the eating of people. A body was just a meal. Clearly, there must be something more to it, or at least I hoped there was. To find out, I figured, I would have to ask a cannibal. And if there was one island where I thought I might find a cannibal, it was Malekula.

UPON INDEPENDENCE in 1980, Vanuatu shed its colonial designation—the New Hebrides—and assumed its current name. Vanuatu derives from *vanua*, the word for "land" in many Pacific languages. Most newly independent nations would take this as just the beginning. The names of towns would change. Street names would no longer honor King Leopold or some other distant tyrant. Islands and provinces would assume their original, precolonial place-names. Not so in Vanuatu. Indeed, our neighborhood in Port Vila still retained the name given to it by American soldiers in World War II: *Nambatri*, pidgin for "number three." *Nambatu* was just down the road, which led to *Nambawan*, or downtown. It was much the same throughout the islands, where many bays, lagoons, points, and even mountains retained the names given to them by Westerners. Even many of the islands themselves kept the names bestowed by the first foreign visitors. Captain Bligh didn't even set foot on the Banks Islands, which he named for Joseph Banks, the naturalist. Of course, he was in a hurry at the time, having recently lost his ship *The Bounty* to Christian Fletcher and his fellow mutineers, and after his open longboat was chased by cannibals when he passed through Fiji, he knew that this was the wrong neighborhood for dillydallying. There have, however, been some modifications to island names. Pedro Fernandez de Quirós, when he landed on Vanuatu's largest island in 1606, believed he had discovered the mythical southern continent, and he named it Australia del Espíritu Santo. The Australia part was dropped, however, when someone found another Australia, and today the island is called Espírítu Santo, or just Santo.

One can understand the reticence of the Ni-Vanuatu when it comes to changing their islands' names. If, for example, the people of a particular island speak twenty languages, there are likely twenty different names for the island, and so settling on a local word for their home is bound to be difficult. Nevertheless, if there is one island where one would think that its inhabitants would make the effort, it would be Malekula. Like so many islands in the South Pacific, Malekula was named by the intrepid Captain Cook, who stumbled upon it in July 1774, during his second great voyage of discovery when he was captain of the *Resolution*. He called the island Mallicullo, and it is generally understood that this was a play on the French expression *mal a cul,* which translates as "pain in the ass." I found this a little fanciful, a little out of character for Captain Cook, who is widely regarded as having been particularly humane and tolerant in his relations with people in the South Pacific. It seemed unlikely that he would name an island in a fit of petulance, but after reading his notes on Malekula, I wasn't so sure. "The people of this country are in general the most Ugly and ill-proportioned of any I

ever saw," he wrote. "They are almost black or rather a dark Chocolate Colour, Slenderly made, not tall, have Monkey faces and wooly
hair . . . We saw but few Women and they were fully as disagreeable
as the Men."

Sadly, the Malekulans did not write, so we do not have any notes
that could tell us what they thought of Captain Cook and his crew,
who had spent the previous two years tightly confined in a rat-
infested wooden ship, much of it spent in the tropics, without access
to a shower or deodorant, and as they were Englishmen in an age
before sunscreen, their skin must have been of particular interest to
Malekulans. "These Creatures are the most Repellent beasts we have
yet encountered," one can imagine a Malekulan writing. "They have
Red skin that flakes and sheds like a serpent, except for the parts that
they cover, which is a Hideous white. Many are Furry like our swine
and they exhibit a most Malodorous stench. They have no Females
among them, and we take them for Sodomites, with an Unnatural
appetite for Buggery."

In the end, Cook did not stay long. Though he was in need of
food and water, the Malekulans had made it clear that they really
rather wished that he and his men would just mosey on and leave
their island. Presumably, they thought Cook was a ghost, and who
could blame them for wanting little to do with the Undead? As they
left, Cook and his officers dined on a couple of fish they had caught,
which caused them to be "seiz'd with Violent pains in the head and
Limbs, so as to be unable to stand, together with a kind of Scorch-
ing heat all over the Skin." Perhaps this was his pain-in-the-ass
moment.

As I made my arrangements for Malekula, it occurred to me that
if I had the choice, I would much rather sail to the island in a rat-
infested wooden ship than fly Vanair. I do not like to fly. A 747 re-
duces me to sweaty palms and heart palpitations. A Twin Otter in a

mountainous third-world country is basically a full-on cardiac event for me. Not long before, a Vanair Twin Otter had crashed into the ocean near Port Vila, downed by a violent squall. Though miraculously four people were able to swim to shore, eight died. A few years earlier, a Vanair Islander had slammed into a mountain on Aneityum. There were no survivors. That's two planes lost by a four-plane airline. I wondered whether I should pack a defibrillator.

At the time, Sylvia was on a business trip to Bali. It's rugged work, international development, but if someone was needed to attend a weeklong conference on coral reefs at a beachside resort in Indonesia, Sylvia was willing to do it. With a week to myself, I had decided to spend it in a hut on a malarial island far away from the resorts on Efate. But as I caught a minibus to the airport I began to regret Sylvia's absence immensely. No man likes to be reduced to a quivering, sobbing wreck in front of his wife, and in the past, whenever we had flown on small planes together, it was that fact alone, I felt, which had prevented the onslaught of panic. I had some dim hopes that I would be flying the ATR, a forty-five-passenger prop plane, the largest in the Vanair fleet, but I knew that those hopes were misplaced. The ATR required a proper runway. Malekula didn't have a proper runway. It had a clearing in the bush. And so I boarded a Twin Otter with about the same enthusiasm I'd feel if I were settling in for a root canal. To my mild surprise, I wasn't the only Westerner aboard. There were two missionaries, a middle-aged couple from Australia. ELDA WOODRUFF, said the man's name tag, and if his black pants and white short-sleeved shirt didn't give it away, the name tag did. They were Mormons. Like me, they were probably hoping to find cannibals, too.

I said a quick prayer to the Mormon god—why not? It couldn't hurt—and soon we were high above the ocean, where the pilot steered a course toward every squall in the greater Vanuatu area. It was remarkable flying. I could see through the cockpit window, and I noticed that if we flew just a little to the left, we would avoid flying through a billowing black cloud, the kind of ominous dark mass that would give even a 747 a good shake. Instead, we plied right through it, lurching wildly, and when we emerged, the pilot immediately turned his plane toward the next squall. Indeed, I believe we may have even turned around to fly through the same squall twice. Needless to say, I had curled myself into a fetal position, closed my eyes, clasped my hands, and spent a long hour muttering, *I am in my safe place,* until the pilot, with a move that would make a kamikaze pilot proud, took us into a steeply pitched dive, engines screaming, and aimed the plane toward a mountain on what I took to be Malekula. Then up we went again, barely cresting a dense growth of trees, thumping in the turbulent air, until suddenly we were following the coastline toward the airport at Norsup, where we landed on a slab of jagged coral. Emerging from the plane with trembling knees, I felt immeasurable relief that the ordeal was over, and then it occurred to me that in five days I would have to do it all over again. This better be an interesting island, I thought, and when I noticed the airport building, I realized that it would be.

The building, which had once been a tidy single-story cinderblock structure, had been reduced to a slab of stones and burnt embers. It was not decayed. It was destroyed, though this did not prevent the Vanair representative from conducting his business. He had set up a table in a roofless room, surrounded by rubble and clucking hens, and there he checked in the passengers who were continuing on to Santo. If this had been the scene in Port Vila, I would have turned around right then, my confidence in Vanair shattered, but this was an outer island, said by many to be the most "primitive" in Vanuatu, and now that I was here, with the terror of air travel behind me, I was feeling positively ebullient, eager to experience the raw Pacific.

I grabbed my backpack, made my way past the chickens and assorted onlookers, and immediately wondered how I was going to get myself to Rose Bay, where I had made arrangements to stay in a guesthouse. There were a couple of battered pickup trucks idling beside the airport, and seeing that there was no one here to take me to the guesthouse, which was some twenty miles north of Norsup, the main village on Malekula, I asked the drivers in my rudimentary Bislama if they were heading in that direction. I knew enough about the outer islands to realize that if there's a vehicle going in your direction, get on, because it could be days before there's another. Soon I found myself in the back of a pickup truck, holding on for dear life as we careened along a gravel road. Past the coconut plantations that surrounded the airport, the gravel gave way to a deeply gutted dirt path, and as we barreled over every pothole, I found it was all I could do to remain inside the truck. How do they do it, I wondered as we passed another pickup fully laden with people. There I was, tucked into a sort of Ninja crouch, my arms encircled around a steel rail, and still I flailed alarmingly, whereas the locals managed to sit on the rim, and not only did they not fall out but they weren't even holding on, just leaning their bodies in accordance with the truck's movement.

After about a half-hour of this, the driver suddenly came to a stop, which nearly sent me hurtling over the hood. His other passenger, a barefoot, bearded man carrying a bushel of yams, emerged from the passenger seat, disappeared up a footpath, and was soon swallowed by the bush. The driver indicated that I could join him in the cab. He didn't have to ask twice. His name was Gerard, and as we proceeded toward Rose Bay, following an increasingly narrow path that cleaved through the jungle, we got to talking. Malekula is predominantly francophone, and so I asked him, in French, about the airport.

"Land dispute," he said. "The landowner wanted more money

from the government. When the government refused to pay, the landowner destroyed the airport building."

"And is this a common way of settling land disputes?" I asked.

"Very common."

Gerard asked me about what I intended to do on Malekula. I mentioned that among the places I hoped to visit was the island of Vao, just off the northeast coast of Malekula. Vao was a kastom island.

"You cannot go to Vao," Gerard said.

"Why not?"

"There is a dispute with the chief. No one is permitted to go to Vao."

"And are there many disputes on Malekula?"

"Many. But do not worry. Peter will take care of you."

Peter was the owner of Rose Bay Bungalows. *Bungalow* might be a rather extravagant word to describe the rudimentary shelters he had constructed, though they were certainly ingenious. It's funny how accustomed one gets to electricity and running water, and as I contemplated the bamboo walls, the mosquito net, and the courtesy kerosene lantern, I marveled at what a different world Vanuatu was outside Port Vila. This wasn't quite as primitive as the outer islands of Kiribati, but I still felt far away from the world beyond the reef.

"Is malaria a big problem here?" I asked.

"Yes," Peter said. "It's a very big problem. And now is the malaria season."

Of course it was.

I immersed myself in a toxic cloud of mosquito repellent and followed Peter as he showed me around. There were several other Gilligan's Island–style bungalows, connected by a series of stone paths that looped through the trees in an amusingly complex manner. Malekula is a remarkably fecund island. Some twenty thousand people live there, and on the drive from the airport, I had wondered where, exactly, were these twenty thousand people, until I peered a little more closely through the trees and realized we were passing through a village. Even the villages were difficult to distinguish from the lush growth that seemed just one rainfall away from swallowing everything. Within minutes of following Peter, I was thoroughly disoriented.

"Dinner will be at six," he informed me. This left a little more than an hour to ramble about.

"I can hear the ocean, Peter. But I can't see it. Could you point the way?"

The beach was just fifty or so yards from where we stood. The sand was an ash-gray ocher color festooned with driftwood and shells. A short distance offshore were two lush islets, Wala and Atchin, both inhabited. Strolling along the beach, I wondered if I could swim here. The air was still and humid, and after the excitement of flying Vanair I fairly ached for a plunge. Normally, I would have dived right in, but Malekula has a well-deserved reputation for shark attacks. Tiger sharks, bull sharks, even great white sharks were known to prowl its waters. About a half-mile farther, I noticed what appeared to be a group of women and children. Curiously, none of the kids were swimming in the ocean, which told me all I needed to know. There were sharks.

I walked toward them, and as I neared the women they waved hello encouragingly. Between us there was a swift-moving stream that emptied into the ocean. How to ford it, I wondered, without drenching my clothes? It was waist deep. Boys were swimming and diving into the freshwater, and the women, who had been fishing with hand lines, gathered with great smiles of amusement, beckoning me across. I paced back and forth, searching for the shallowest crossing point. Giving up, I marched in, and noticing the mirth and laughter of my spectators as I emerged with sopping shorts, I felt very pleased that I was able to provide the afternoon entertainment.

"Alo, alo," they said.

Most of the boys were naked, and they stopped their play for a moment. "Whiteman," they whispered. I stifled an urge to say "Boo."

"Yu tok-tok engglis?" I asked no one in particular. A half-dozen fingers pointed toward a shy young woman carrying a toddler. Her name was Sally, and she hailed from Paama, a small island to the east of Malekula. Her husband was from the village just up the hill.

"Is this a Small Namba village or a Big Namba village?" I asked her.

"This is a Small Namba village," Sally said as her little boy and I made googly eyes at each other.

Though twenty-eight languages are spoken on Malekula, most of the island's inhabitants are roughly divided among Small Nambas and Big Nambas. I found it curious that a people's identity could be defined by the size of the leaf that men wore wrapped around their penises. And what exactly was the difference? Did the Big Nambas have more to hide, or were the Small Nambas just a little prouder of their members? Historically, the Small Nambas and the Big Nambas were engaged in constant warfare. The hatred seemed rather perplexing to me. "Hey, look," I imagined a warrior saying. "He's got a tiny leaf on his dick. Let's eat him." Clearly, this needed further investigating, but I sensed that this wasn't quite the right forum for such a line of inquiry, and instead I asked about the fishing.

"Only small fish," she said, showing me her catch, a handful of silvery fish, each no more than three inches long.

"Are there any sharks here?" I asked, getting to the crux of the matter.

"Yes. There are sharks."

"Have there been any attacks recently?"

"Yes. A man was killed off Vao," she said, pointing in the direction of the island, which lay a little ways to the north of Rose Bay. "And there was another who was killed off Atchin, and another off Wala." Atchin and Wala were within hailing distance of where we stood. "There was also one whiteman who was bitten off Wala."

"Really," I said.

"Yes. He was bitten in the leg, but it wasn't a shark."

"What was it?"

"A barracuda."

Well, that settled it. The ocean was placid and beckoning and alluring. And it was full of monsters. Nothing could induce me to take a swim here. On Tarawa, I had happily swum in an ocean that functioned as a toilet. True, that could kill you too. But it hardly compared to the terror of seeing a fifteen-foot tiger shark barreling toward your naked torso.

"Are there saltwater crocodiles to worry about too?" That would complete the tableau of oceanic terror for me. Crocodiles periodically swam down to Vanuatu from the Solomon Islands.

She laughed. "No, there are no crocodiles."

"Well, thank goodness for that."

I gave a thoughtful glance at the ocean, wondering about all that lurked below the surface, when I noticed something odd. The presence of Wala and Atchin and the encircling population of sharks suggested there was a coral reef. And if there was a reef, then there were fish, fish much larger than the meager pickings the women had managed to catch with their hand lines onshore. But there weren't any canoes or boats of any kind. No one was on the water fishing, which seemed very strange to me. On Malekula people lived off what they caught and grew themselves, and so it seemed peculiar that no one was taking advantage of what I assumed would be a bountiful catch.

"Do the men here go out to catch fish beyond the reef?" I asked.

"Not very often," Sally said.

"So who does the fishing?"

"We do."

"And the gardening?"

"The women."

"And the women take care of the children?"

"Yes," she laughed.

"So what do the men do here?"

"They tell stories. And drink kava."

There's the good life.

"Look," Sally said, pointing behind me. "Your friend is here."

My friend? I had a friend on Malekula? Across the stream, my friend, a fleshy Ni-Vanuatu man of about forty with a bald dome that glistened in the sun, waved, encouraging me to cross. What, I thought, my friend doesn't want to get his shorts wet? I bade good-bye to Sally and marched back through the stream to greet my friend, who was sitting on the sand, resting his legs.

"I am George," he said curtly. "Do you have a Lonely Planet?"

I did indeed have the Lonely Planet guide to Vanuatu. We had brought it out from the U.S. Remarkably, they had a chapter on Malekula, which I had read thoroughly, highlighting all the references—and there were many—to the dangers posed by sharks.

"Turn to page one-fourteen," he said. "Do you see?" He jabbed at the page. "That's me."

The entry to which he referred read, in its entirety: "In the village on Wala Island, George's Guestroom is small, for one or two people."

"Well, George," I said. "I'm pleased to meet you."

We ambled along the beach back toward Rose Bay Bungalows, which was also described on page 114 of the Lonely Planet guide to Vanuatu, just below the entry for George's Guestroom. "Traditional bungalows," it read, along with "intoxicating surroundings" and, most important, "the food is good." I thought of suggesting to George that it might be time to hire a new publicist.

"So what do you want to do on Malekula?" George asked. He was, apparently, the self-appointed guide for this part of the island.

"Well, I think I'd like to talk to a cannibal, if there happens to be one around."

George nodded. "Yes, we eat the man here."

Really.

"In time past."

"Ah . . . well, is there anyone around who remembers eating a man?"

"Yes," George said. "There is an old man on Wala Island. He eat the man."

"Do you think I might be able to talk to him?" I asked hopefully. I hadn't the remotest idea of what exactly I would say to him. Cultural sensitivity and cannibalism, I found, did not blend easily.

George indicated that it wouldn't be a problem. This pleased me, and I happily agreed to all his suggestions for enhancing my stay on Malekula—kastom dancing, a trip to Wala Island. What I really wanted to do, however, was to learn as much about cannibalism as possible. I had read that there was an old cannibal village up in the hills above Wala.

"Botko," George said. "It is a Small Namba cannibal village."

"Could I go up there?"

"I will see."

George joined me for dinner, canned corned beef and rice with slices of pumpkin and papaya, prepared by Peter's daughter. I made a mental note to send a letter to Lonely Planet. This was the typical outer island grub I had been hoping to avoid eating. It was, in fact, that promising phrase "the food is good" that had induced me to stay here. What was it about Pacific Islanders and their canned corned beef? Paul Theroux theorized that the people of Oceania enjoyed corned beef because it reminded them of human flesh. Could be, I thought as I picked at the gristle. I washed the victuals down with rainwater. George and Peter spoke together in their language. It was quite a serious discussion, I gathered. At length, Peter said, "You want to speak to one old man who eat the man?"

"Yes," I said, wiping my mouth. "If it's not too much trouble. I'm curious about the traditional customs on Malekula."

"That old man," Peter said, "he died last month."

"I'm sorry to hear it." I paused for a moment. "Is there anyone in this area who may have witnessed the eating of a man? Could I speak to that person?"

"Yes," George said. "There is also an old woman on Wala Island who saw her father eat the man."

"Do you think I might be able to speak to her?"

"Yes," George said. "I will arrange it."

He and Peter discussed the matter further. Something was afoot, I deduced. Either George really wanted to get me over to Wala Island, or Peter really didn't want me talking to cannibals. I left them to their discussion, thanking them effusively for their hospitality, and made my way back to my bamboo bungalow.

Within moments I was pathetically lost. It was a moonless, overcast night. I had forgotten to bring the courtesy kerosene lantern, and I stumbled about in the darkness for a small eternity. Somehow I had lost the footpath. I walked into trees. I had a half-dozen thrilling encounters with spiderwebs. I found myself inches from toppling down a steep gully. *Okay,* I thought, listening to the waves fracturing on the beach. *The ocean is there. If I turn around and walk diagonally away from the ocean, I will reach the food hut, where Peter and George will be able to set me aright.* With a triumphant yelp, I eventually stumbled upon the food hut, only to encounter more darkness. Life on Malekula, I discovered, ended at sunset. Cautiously, I reentered the forest, straining my sensory capabilities as I sought to stay on the footpath. Whenever I was in doubt, I did a sort of crab walk, using my hands to figure out the path's parameters. I did, of course, finally find my bungalow, where I spent a good ten minutes wrestling with a mosquito net, and when I heard the buzz of a mosquito ringing in my ear, I thought, *Please be on the outside of the net.* And then I smacked myself to sleep.

THE FOLLOWING MORNING George led me up a bush trail to a dusty kastom village in the hills above Wala Bay.

"Here you will see the kastom dancing," he said as I settled on a bench. "The men will wear their nambas."

In his ship's journal, Captain Cook described the nambas worn on Malekula:

> *The Men go naked, it can hardly be said they cover their Natural parts, the Testicles are quite exposed, but they wrap a piece of cloth or leafe round the yard which they tye up to the belly to a cord or bandage which they wear round the waist just under the Short Ribs and over the belly and so tight that it was a wonder to us how they could endure it.*

This was my thinking exactly. How did they endure it? Just watching them dance made me wince. The dance seemed to involve much stomping and jogging. The chief, a slender man with a gray beard, provided percussion by pounding a tam-tam, or slit drum. The dance leader had a crown of bird feathers on his head, and periodically he led the others in a sort of swooning dive. It was meant to evoke the flight of an eagle, but frankly, the naked buttocks and bouncing testicles had a way of interrupting the image. It was remarkably different from the dancing I had known in Kiribati, a Micronesian country. As in Polynesia, the dancing there is very formal, highly choreographed, and often subtle. The dancing I was witnessing here seemed more of the make-it-up-as-I-go-along school. The next dance, however, I recognized immediately. It was the hokey-pokey. *Put your left foot in, put your right foot out, now take it all out and shake it all about.* I couldn't stop wincing. I made a mental note to send a carton of boxer shorts to the village as a humanitarian gesture.

The women then did a sitting dance that celebrated the yam harvest. The older women wore a thatch skirt and nothing else. The younger women—and I don't want to suggest for a minute that I had been looking forward to seeing their breasts—wrapped their breasts in cloth, a circumstance I attributed to the insidious influence of missionaries on the young. Afterward, the dancers stood in a line. I shook their hands one by one, feeling very much like the queen of England visiting her far-flung subjects.

"The men," George told me, "live on this side of the village." He gestured toward several longhouses. "And the women live on the other side," he said, pointing to the huts opposite the village clearing.

"What about the married couples?" I asked.

"It is the same. The men stay on this side, and the women on the other."

"But what if they want to . . . you know . . . um, make babies?"

"When the man want to sleep with the woman," George said, "they go into the bush."

I tried imagining the arrangement. "Hey, honey. How about

midnight under the banyan tree? What do you say? A little rumble in the jungle?"

"What about the children?" I asked. "Where do they live?"

"The children live with the women. But after the boys are circumcised, they live with the men."

"And when are boys circumcised?"

"Sometime between the ages of nine and twelve," he said. "It is a very important ceremony. Many pigs are killed."

George showed me the longhouse where boys were brought after they were circumcised. It was adorned with masks and fern sculptures. It had a dirt floor and a thatch ceiling. "The boys are circumcised as a group, and after they are circumcised, they stay here for ten days. It is very difficult. It is the first time the boys are away from their mothers. And at night, we bother them."

"You bother them?"

"Yes. We bang on the walls, and we howl. The boys are very frightened. They think there are ghosts. And sometimes we go in and kick sand on their wounds. It is very painful."

"Well, that's not very nice."

"No," George said, recollecting his own circumcision. "It is not nice. But it is the custom. Afterward, the boys are men and they live with the other men."

What a curious way to live, I thought. One thing seemed clear, though. One certainly didn't want to be a penis on Malekula.

IN THE AFTERNOON, George took me to Wala Island. We paddled an outrigger canoe across Wala Bay—or, rather, I paddled an outrigger canoe. George steered. Paddling two grown men into the teeth of an incoming tide and up and over the ocean swell under the blistering midday sun left me sweating and panting from the exertion. There was a fine white sand beach on Wala Island, and when we arrived, I gave in and dived into the warm turquoise water.

"Maybe not such a good idea to swim there," George said from the beach.

Easy for you to say, I thought. Next time I'm steering. "Why, George? This is wonderful."

I was in clear, shallow water above a sandy bottom, facing Malekula, not the open ocean.

"Maybe you should swim there," George suggested, pointing to the water alongside a dock that jutted out several yards.

"Whatever you say." I was as pleased as I could be to be swimming. The South Pacific, after all, is the South Pacific, and sun, palm trees, a splendid beach, and clear, warm, gorgeous water, I find, are irresistible. I did an easy backstroke toward the pier.

"What are you looking for?" I asked George. He was standing on the pier, scanning the water.

"Nothing."

"Seriously, George," I said. "What are you looking for?"

"The water is very deep over there."

"So? I can swim."

"There are many sharks living there."

If there were six words that could ruin a swim in the South Pacific, George had found them. I was out in a heartbeat. I did not know it then, but shortly before I arrived on Malekula, a seven-year-old girl had been killed by a tiger shark. This had occurred not one hundred yards from where I swam, off Atchin, an islet a short swim from Wala Island. The shark had severed the child's leg.

We walked around Wala, a circumnavigation that took twenty minutes. The villagers were slumbering in the shade and hardly gave me a glance, which I found a little peculiar. Malekula and the islets that circled it were not often visited by Westerners.

"George," I said. "What are all these stands for?" The entire periphery of the island had the appearance of an empty market.

"For the cruise ship."

Say what? "Did you say cruise ship?"

"Yes. During the season, a cruise ship comes every six weeks. Not now. Now is cyclone season."

I cannot express how disheartened I was to learn this. Here I was, enduring perilous flights in rickety third-world airplanes, canned corned beef, and mosquito nets, all so that I could experience life on one of the most isolated, unchanging islands in the world, and now there were cruise ships.

"They come for two hours," George said. "And they buy souvenirs. So we make souvenirs now."

"And make lots of money?"

"Yes." George laughed. "Dollars, not vatu."

At that moment, a boat powered off carrying five exuberant youths, who steered it in the nautical equivalent of a drunk man's stagger.

"Ha-ha," George laughed. "They are going to buy the beer."

The only place on Malekula where beer was available was in Norsup. I had checked. It would take the boys the rest of the afternoon to acquire it. What a waste, I thought. Kava offered so much more bang for the buck, which got me thinking.

"George," I said. "Do you think I can drink some kava this evening?"

"You like kava?"

"George, me likem kava tumas."

That evening, in a family compound near the shoreline back on Malekula, I found myself sitting among people who seemed oddly familiar to me. "Hey," I said to one young man. And then in French, "I recognize you."

"I was wondering if you would recognize me," he said. By this he meant, *I was wondering if you'd recognize me with my clothes on.* He was the dancer with the plume of feathers. Several of the other dancers had joined me on the benches in the nakamal. An elderly man was grinding the kava roots. Tending the children on the periphery were several of the women dancers.

"I thought you lived in the kastom village."

"Now we live down here," he said. His name was Philip.

"So who lives up in the village?"

"The chief and his sons. But we go for our ceremonies."

Interesting, I thought. Looking around, I suddenly noticed a cascade of ropes among the trees. Attached were sharp, dangling hooks. "What's that for?" I asked Philip.

"For catching bats."

"Ah . . . and why would you catch bats?"

"For eating."

"I see. And do bats make for good eating?"

"Yes," Philip said. Better than corned beef, no doubt.

George joined us on the bench. "You can go to Botko tomorrow," he said.

"It is a very special place," Philip added.

"Will you be coming, George?"

"No." He laughed. "It is too far for me. But you will learn many things in Botko."

"George," I said. "You had mentioned that there was an old woman on Wala Island who had witnessed her father eating the man."

"Yes, yes," George said. "But she died too. Last month."

Clearly, the previous month on Malekula had not been a good

one for those with firsthand knowledge of cannibalism. Or George had been joshing with me all along. Or, and I thought this was most likely, my interest in cannibalism had come across as a little unseemly to the powers that be on Malekula. I couldn't blame them. It was like meeting a German for the first time and asking them to explain their nation's curious tradition of killing people in concentration camps.

Philip handed me a shell of kava. I can't say I recall much of what happened subsequently, except that I felt at one with the Small Nambas of Malekula.

MY GUIDE UP into the highlands was Rose-Marie, the nineteen-year-old daughter of Chief Jamino, the guardian of Botko. How hard could this trek be, I wondered, if my guide is wearing a Harry Potter shirt, a sarong, and flip-flops? Of course, she also had a machete, but I figured everybody on Malekula carried a machete. It was the accessory of choice. Looking back, I can now say that the five hours it took to hike up to Botko were the most excruciatingly difficult five hours I have ever spent on my feet. We left shortly after dawn, following a well-traveled bush trail that meandered inland. I had filled two plastic bottles with rainwater, which I carried in a backpack. Soon I added two coconuts and a melon that were kindly given to us by a man we encountered on the trail. If there is anything more uncomfortable to carry on one's back than two bouncing coconuts and a melon, I have yet to experience it. As we climbed up the first of what would prove to be a seemingly endless series of steep hills, following a path evident only to Rose-Marie, who hacked our way forward with her machete, I pleaded for a break. "Would you like a coconut?" I asked, speaking in French.

"No, thank you," she said.

"Rose-Marie, if you don't drink this coconut, I am going to hurl it off this mountain. I have ill feelings toward these coconuts."

With a deft tap of the machete, Rose-Marie opened up the nuts. I took a greedy slurp, downing the milk in one go, and moved on to my water bottle, chugging through half a liter. I asked Rose-Marie if she wanted some water. It was particularly hot and humid. Indeed, I was quite amazed by the quantity of sweat seeping through my pores. "Non, merci," she said. I wondered what the French word for camel was.

Not long after, my mind turned to the French word for goat. *Chèvre?* I found myself on some particularly taxing slope, clutching onto a tree root, wondering how on earth I was going to scale this muddy face, when suddenly I saw Rose-Marie scamper up the incline without pause, seemingly without exertion, without even a hint of perspiration, as I stood there gasping for breath, oozing puddles of sweat. The most disheartening part of the climb, however, was that with each crest of a hill there followed a perilous descent. One moment I'd find myself on a ridge, peering through man-high grass, admiring the view, and thinking, Well, we must be close now, and suddenly Rose-Marie, with a few swift hacks of the machete, would forge a path that led *down,* back into a dense chirping, mocking forest. We'd ford a stream, and then up we went again. I was expelling copious amounts of sweat. Indeed, I began to worry about dehydration, and it was with particular amazement that I noticed that Rose-Marie's brow wasn't even glistening.

"Rose-Marie," I panted. "How often do you climb up to Botko?"

"Every day," she said.

You are fucking joking, I thought. I felt that I was reasonably fit, perhaps not quite in peak form, but not the sort of person who withers in a typical hike. Compared to Rose-Marie I was a sack of potatoes. To do such a hike, each and every day, without even breaking a sweat when it's ninety-some degrees with humidity to match, is a remarkable feat of athleticism. Before I had a chance to feel old, however, we emerged through a clump of trees and I beheld a most welcome sight: a village. Not just any village, but a remarkably neat and tidy village surrounded by numerous fruit trees.

I was welcomed by Chief Jamino, an imposing man wearing a faded and stained pink oxford shirt with a white collar, a discard, no doubt from the Gordon Gecko era of Wall Street. He guided me to a mat, where I more or less collapsed into an unceremonious heap, panting and sweating without shame. I must have made quite an impression, for no sooner had I taken my place on the mat than the village women appeared with coconuts, sugarcane, and grapefruit. My empty water bottles were filled with rainwater, and it wasn't long before I began to feel restored.

Chief Jamino, speaking through a translator, explained that this was a village of seven brothers, of whom he was the eldest. Forty-nine people lived here, the families of the seven brothers. They were the guardians of Botko. It was a very pleasant village. The homes were well-constructed with wood and thatch and obviously cared for. There was a rainwater tank. The grass was kept low. The air was much cooler than on the coast. And the villagers, I was gratified to see, appeared in blooming health.

Chief Jamino went off to tend to something, and his place on the mat was taken by Elise, a vivacious woman in her twenties who spoke English. "When the chief is here," she said, "I must be someplace else. When I am in my home, he cannot come in. When he is on the mat, I must be someplace else. I am his daughter-in-law. It is the custom. I wanted to explain why I did not greet you at first."

This seemed rather rigorous for such a small village, until I saw Chief Jamino rejoin us on the adjoining mat, which apparently was a satisfactory arrangement. For lunch, we had laplap, a mush of manioc and coconut cream wrapped in taro leaves and cooked in an earth oven over heated rocks. This particular laplap came with freshwater prawns, which pleased me, because, frankly, I hate laplap. It looks like vomit and the taste is insipidly sweet, but I ate it with gratitude, because at least it was something other than corned beef.

"What is that spear for?" I asked the chief's son-in-law, pointing to an enormous spear leaning against a tree.

"We use it for killing wild pigs."

"And how big are the pigs?"

"About this big," he said, drawing a length on the ground, suggesting that these were gargantuan pigs.

"And they have tusks?"

"Yes, they have tusks."

"And are they dangerous?" I asked, wondering what else I had to look forward to on the hike back down to Wala Bay.

"Only when you are trying to kill them. Then they are very dangerous."

"Well, if I see one," I said, "I think I'll climb a tree."

"But you must choose the right tree and climb very high," Elise added, "because the pig will stand on his legs and jump after you."

Great, I thought. Giant jumping pigs.

But before heading down, I still had, alas, another climb ahead of me. Women were forbidden to visit the cannibal settlement, and so I said good-bye to Elise, Rose-Marie, and the others and joined the men for the march up to Botko. We passed kava bushes and more fruit trees, and soon we were back in the green forest, following a path that led straight up. They are goat-people, I thought as I pulled myself up, clasping onto tree roots and branches. We scrambled over rocks and the sharp, fallen detritus of the forest. I was the only one wearing shoes. Finally, we stopped.

"This is the water cistern," said Chief Jamino, speaking through his son-in-law. There was a gaggle of large rocks through which a small stream trickled. Finally, I thought. The water source. We must be close. We hiked on. A half-hour later, just as I was frothing with exasperation—Where the hell is this cannibal village?—we paused in front of a large, flat slab of rock. The chief spoke.

"This is the altar where the pigs were sacrificed." No event of consequence occurs in Vanuatu without a pig sacrifice. "And this," he said, reaching into a crevice below the altar, "was a very great chief."

Hello.

In his hands, Chief Jamino was cradling a skull. "He was a god. He discovered how to make fire. Do you see this stone?" he said, pointing to a boulder. "He make the fire like this." The chief returned the skull to its place, rather unceremoniously I thought, and hopped on top of the boulder. With a stick he proceeded to exuberantly demonstrate how fire was made. He scraped the wood back and forth through a well-defined groove in the boulder. In a shallow indentation he had placed some kindling, and after five or so minutes of frantic scraping and blowing, smoke appeared.

"When did this great chief live?" I asked.

"A long time ago," Chief Jamino said. "A hundred years past."

Well, I certainly didn't want to take anything away from the great chief, but it did seem to me that he was a trifle late in joining the rest of humanity in discovering how to make fire.

Stepping down, Chief Jamino reached into another crevice below the altar and retrieved another, better-preserved skull. "This was his son. And this was the son's tusk. He wore it like a bracelet, like this," he said, trying on the pig tusk. He placed the skull and the tusk back into its crevice, then reached for yet another, even better preserved skull. "This was the son's son."

I pondered the skulls for a moment. Very curious, I asked: "How did you get the heads?"

"After they died, we buried them standing up, just up to their necks. And when the heads fell off, we brought them here."

This was almost too ghastly for me to envisage. How long would it take for a head to snap off? A month? Two? What about the flies? Did anyone trip over the heads? That first skull looked a little battered.

We moseyed on. The village, what remained of it, was densely overgrown. Was it always so? I asked.

"No," Chief Jamino said. "This was all cleared. The village was abandoned because it was too far from the water source. But we keep it overgrown because we don't want other tribes to find it. They will disturb it."

"You mean the Big Nambas?"

"Yes, the Big Nambas."

Then he related an interesting tale. A few months earlier, the chief of a Big Namba village asked Chief Jamino for a curious favor. His village, the Big Namba chief said, was disturbed. The spirits were unhappy. Ghosts were tormenting the people. The villagers were suffering one misfortune after another. Could they please have some of their bones back? he asked. The chief felt this would appease the spirits. "So we gave him some bones, and now the village is peaceful again."

"And do you keep many bones here?" I asked.

"Yes, there are many bones. You will see."

We walked on to what was once the village chief's throne, a stone-slab easy chair that rested on a rise. "The chief sit here, and the assistant chief stand there," Chief Jamino said, gesturing. "Like in a parliament."

Below, in a clearing surrounded by enormous banyan trees, was where the village ceremonies occurred. "This is where the captured men were brought," Chief Jamino informed me. "We give them kava. And then they were made to dance."

Dance?

"And then we kill them."

"How?" I asked.

"With clubs," Chief Jamino replied.

"And then what?"

"And then we eat them."

Well, I thought, here was my chance to get the nitty-gritty details of cannibalism. I asked the chief how they prepared the men they were about to eat. How was the flesh cooked?

"We cut the man into small pieces and put it inside the bamboo. And then we roast it over the fire."

"Did you use any seasoning?" Well, I was curious.

"No, only the meat."

"Were there any parts of the man you didn't eat?" I asked. If I were a cannibal, I figured, there would certainly be a few parts I wouldn't touch.

"No," the chief said. "We eat the whole man." I absorbed this. Then Chief Jamino added: "But not the woman. We don't eat the woman, and the woman don't eat the man. The woman was used as a messenger from village to village."

Well, I thought. There's at least one upside to being a woman in Vanuatu.

Chief Jamino led me to a large pile of what I took to be stones. "This is where we put the bones," the chief said. And so they were. The bones stretched the length of a school bus, stacked waist high.

These were the remains of the Big Nambas that the Small Nambas had devoured. "This is a thigh bone," the chief said, plucking out a calcified limb.

Finally, I asked Chief Jamino what I had come all this way for. "Why did you eat people? Was it a ritual, where you had to destroy an enemy completely so that he doesn't attack you in the spirit world?"

"No," he said. "In former times before the whiteman come, there were many men but not much meat. And so we kill the men for eating."

And that's all I really wanted to know.

CHAPTER 7

In which the author experiences his first cyclone, causing him to reconsider his position on Nature—whether he's for it or against it—and after a terrifying encounter with a giant centipede seems to have settled the issue, his wife gives him News, which only complicates the matter further.

I HAD ALWAYS BEEN FOND OF NATURE. PROVOCATIVE AND outlandish as that might seem, it's true. That fondness, however, didn't mean I had any great desire to climb a twenty-five-thousand-foot mountain—where's the fun in oxygen depletion?—or dogsled across the frozen tundra. I just liked knowing that nature was there, out there, somewhere. Sitting in a heated living room, watching the nature channel on television, I'd find myself hoping that the animals of the world were all as comfortable as I was. If there was anything I could do for them, I'd be happy to send a check.

In Vanuatu, however, it doesn't take one long to realize that nature might not be so benign. There are no koala bears on these islands. There are, however, sharks. And moray eels too. One day, we had been snorkeling above a coral reef in Mele Bay. I had finally mastered the skill of diving ten feet or so below the surface without inhaling copious amounts of water, and as I plunged to get a closer look at the angelfish clustered in the coral I was startled to find myself face-to-face with a moray eel. If there is a more frightening-looking beast in the world, I hope never to encounter it. This was five feet of electrically charged muscle attached to a face not even a mother could love. Immediately I swallowed a gallon of seawater.

"Moray eel," I sputtered once I had reached the surface.

"Did you see the jellyfish?" Sylvia asked. I had seen it, a translucent blob of poison riding the current. A few moments later, as we swam back to shore, we found ourselves giving a wide berth to a brightly banded venomous sea snake.

It was the centipedes in Vanuatu, however, that had me rethinking my affinity for nature. These creatures—*insect* is such an inadequate word—terrified me. It was the cat who had noticed the first one. He had been given to us by our friend Adam, who had called one day and said, "I know just what you need."

"No you don't."

"Yes I do. What you need is a kitten."

"Adam," I said, "I do not want a kitten."

"Excellent. I'll be right over."

"No, Adam, seriously. I do not want a kitten. I am a kitten hater."

"Fantastic. You're going to love this kitten."

"Please don't do this to me. Just because you have been grossly negligent with your cat . . . what's her name again?"

"Ms. Muggles."

"Just because you have allowed Ms. Muggles to become a shameless fornicator—"

"Hey, that's Ms. Muggles you're talking about."

"Adam, please, no kittens."

"Great. I'll be right over."

We called him Pip. Or, rather, I called him Pip. Sylvia called him Your Cat, as in Your Cat just shit on the floor again. In Kiribati, dogs and cats had intuited that, unlike the I-Kiribati, we were unlikely to kill them, and so eventually we had found ourselves hosting a cat and a half-dozen dogs. Sylvia did not want to repeat the experience. Port Vila too had its share of wild dogs and cats. Sylvia sensed—perhaps correctly—that word would get around in the animal community that we were pushovers and soon we'd be feeding and cleaning up after a dozen strays.

Like most kittens, Pip was spirited and affectionate. I daresay he may have even been cute. A black and white ball of fur, he was particularly talkative. While I worked on my book, he'd spend his time mewing at the various lizards and spiders that periodically stopped by for a visit. Now and then, to amuse myself, I'd lift Pip up to the ceiling where the lizards had crawled out of the reach of his claws. He'd get a good sniff of lizard, and then I'd set him down and watch him scamper up furniture and make spectacular, though futile, leaps into the air, straining to reach the reptiles. You had no idea, did you, that the writing life could be so exciting.

One morning, however, I was gamely trying to ignore the cat. As was his habit, he leapt up onto the dining table where I worked on my laptop. Typically, Pip enjoyed walking on the keyboard and leaving his print on my manuscript—*gtyhjb* was a favorite contribution. I went to shove him off and, unusually for him, he drew his claws, embedding them in the wooden table.

"No, Pip," I admonished. "You can't do that. We're renters."

Meeeoooowww, he howled. He curled his back. His fur stood straight up, as if he had been playing with the electric socket.

"Off, Pip." I picked him up, intending to set him down, and that's when I saw it. A centipede.

Until I saw this particular critter, I had always thought that all centipedes were like those small hundred-legged insects one periodically encounters in North America. On a nuisance scale, a centipede, at least in my experience, ranked far below a mouse, perhaps just a fraction higher than a cricket. A Vanuatu centipede, however, is a different beast altogether. On the nuisance scale, I'd put it up there with a rattlesnake. A Vanuatu centipede is, to begin with, a carnivore. Yes, that's right. Vanuatu centipedes eat meat. Now, I'm no entomologist, but you'd think that fact alone would be enough to bump it out of the insect classification. Second, they are venomous. They kill their prey by injecting it with venom, and have two pincers near their head designed for this very purpose. And then there's this: Their legs are venomous too. Centipedes can have upwards of three hundred legs. Ponder that, if you will. Now, three hundred legs, of course, need to be connected to something— something large enough to carry three hundred legs. You might conclude, then, and rightly so, that Vanuatu centipedes are big, very big. They can grow to be more than a foot long. And they are nearly indestructible. You may think that you've solved the problem by chopping a centipede in two, but in fact, what you have just done is create two angry, scurrying missiles of poison.

And, as I was now discovering, the centipedes in Vanuatu are hideous to behold. I had leapt on top of the table and joined Pip in contemplating the horror that was scampering across the floor. This particular centipede was nearly a foot long. Even a ladybug of those dimensions would have sent me scooting toward high ground. A Vanuatu centipede, however, does not have pretty coloring. It looks remarkably like the Darth Vader of the insect world, armored and menacing, exuding malice. This, I agreed with Pip, was trouble.

Just then the telephone rang. "Why don't you get it, Pip?"

The cat wasn't leaving the table. He stalked and paced with an upturned tail, mewing and moaning, and it was clear that he expected me to deal with the bug. Here, I thought, was a perfectly fine opportunity for the cat to finally capture an animal, but Pip, alas, had been seized by a primal fear. "It's actually a lizard," I told him, but he paid me no mind.

The telephone kept ringing. *Hang up already,* I thought. *I've got a little problem slithering between me and the phone.* The centipede was in no hurry. Its innumerable legs moved it a few feet in one direction, where it would pause and rise up, sensors sensing, and then it would amble a few feet in another direction. It was like watching the world's scariest Slinky. But this Slinky could *move,* if it so chose. There's a lot of propulsion available when you have a hundred-plus legs.

Still the telephone rang.

I descended from the table. It had been creaking ominously. I tiptoed around the room, hugging the walls, maintaining eye contact with the loathsome critter at all times.

"Hello!" I yelped.

"You're not going to believe what's coming," Sylvia began, then stopped. "Are you all right? You sound funny."

"Yeah . . . well . . . I'm being stared down by a centipede."

"So kill it," she said.

"No, you don't understand," I said, climbing on top of the couch. "It's a very large centipede."

"Just grab a paper towel," Sylvia advised.

"Paper towel?" I bleated. "I'll call you back later."

I hung up the phone, bounded into the bedroom, and shut the door. Could the centipede get under the door? I wondered. It was, I estimated, about two inches thick. Yes, probably. I dashed into the closet and grabbed my jeans, as yet unworn in the tropics. I quickly put them on. Then I reached for socks, also unworn. I tucked the jeans into the socks. Then I put on the heavy work boots I had brought to Vanuatu for reasons I could no longer remember. So attired, I reemerged into the tiled living room, the kill zone. The hunted would become the hunter.

The phone rang.

"What?" I barked.

"Be really, really careful with that centipede," Sylvia said. "I mentioned it to the people at work. Did you know that they're poisonous? One bite, they said, is enough to kill a child."

"Paper towel, then?"

"No! Don't use a paper towel."

"I'll call you back." I hung up the phone.

I tentatively approached the centipede. It stopped ambling. It seemed to sense that something was amiss. I raised my foot. Suddenly, it dashed. I squealed pathetically and jumped on top of the couch.

The phone rang.

"Did you kill it?" Sylvia asked.

"No. I haven't had a chance. I've been on the phone."

"You have to crush all of it," she informed me. "If you only smash half of it, the other half lives on."

I hung up.

Once again, I stalked the centipede. It had stopped in the middle of the room. I moved along the walls until I was behind the beast. The cat, still on the table, wailed. Inching forward, I raised my boot. I stomped it down just as the centipede bolted. I crushed its tail with a sickening *splat*. The rest of the centipede scurried on, now panicked and in a bad temper. I brought my other foot down. The centipede splattered with a grotesque crack, spewing copious amounts of centipede innards. And then I kept stomping. *Splat! Splat! Splat!*

It was probably dead, I thought. To make sure, I flattened it some more. *Splat!* It stank horribly. I had never smelled anything so noxious. Not even the cat would approach it.

"A lot of help you were."

The phone rang.

"Did you kill it?" Sylvia asked.

"Yes. I have defended the hearth."

I spent a moment recounting the adventure.

"Do you think there are more?" Sylvia wondered.

This was not a thought I wanted to linger on. Was this centipede a lone wolf among his kind, a distant wanderer, lost from his companions? Or were we living with a den of centipedes? Quite likely it was the latter. The splattered centipede was certainly an anomaly in one way. Centipedes are nocturnal creatures, preferring the darkness. Were there in reality dozens of centipedes wandering about while we slept, doing scary centipede things? Could I ever sleep again?

"Well, the reason I called the first time," Sylvia continued, "was to let you know that there's a cyclone forming just north of the Torres Islands."

So much excitement already, and it wasn't even ten in the morning. I looked outside. It was sunny and calm, though oppressively hot. I have, I confess, a slight weather fetish. Few things make me happier than a blizzard or a spectacular thunderstorm. I had once even contemplated spending a summer chasing tornadoes. In Washington, whenever there was a hurricane pummeling Florida, I'd eagerly watch the news, envying the brave, brave TV correspondents, reporting that the wind was picking up and any moment now their umbrellas were sure to fail. There was always a shot of people merrily goofing around on the beach in Key West, people who had ignored the evacuation orders and were carelessly enjoying the scene as the winds increased from gale to hurricane strength. *Drunken idiots* is what most people called them. I saw them as fellow travelers.

Cyclones are hurricanes, and just as hurricanes in the Atlantic are named, so too are cyclones in the South Pacific. Ours was to be called Paula, and as it gathered strength in the Coral Sea northwest of Vanuatu, I followed its progress with a perverse sense of anticipation. Though Vanuatu averages two or three cyclones a year, there had been an unusual dearth of them in the region recently. The Ni-Vanuatu I spoke with, not unreasonably, thought that this was a good thing. Everyone spoke of Cyclone Uma, which had walloped Vanuatu in 1987, causing considerable damage. Scores of boats had been lost in Vila Harbor. The metal lampposts, I was confidently informed, had been bent in half. Many of the downtown roofs had been shorn off. The villages, of course, suffered even more cruelly. The people on the outer islands had taken shelter under the massive roots of banyan trees, the age-old cyclone shelter, only to return to find that their villages of thatch no longer existed. Shelter, however, was easily replaced. It doesn't take long to build a traditional home using locally available materials. More difficult, however, was replacing the fruit trees that had been lost, and upon which a good deal of the country's population depended for sustenance.

I certainly didn't wish for a repeat of Cyclone Uma. I was hoping for a middling cyclone, the kind that would offer optimum weather drama while producing, ideally, no damage whatsoever. I wasn't sure if such a cyclone existed, but if it did, I wanted to experience it.

Over the next few days, the weather became unbearably sticky and humid, a sure precursor to a storm. There wasn't a cloud anywhere, and yet everything was damp and soppy. The heat and humidity were such that we even considered turning on the window unit air conditioner in our bedroom. This required considerable fortitude on our part. Since our arrival, three geckoes had somehow managed to die deep within its bowels. I had disassembled as much of the unit as I dared and scraped out what I could of the lizards' carcasses. But much remained, slowly, ever so slowly, decomposing beside our bed.

"I can't take this heat anymore," Sylvia said one night as we lay side by side, sweating in the darkness. "Let's turn on the air conditioner."

I closed the windows, sealing the room, and turned the unit on. It clanked and thudded and groaned and eventually began to whir, suffusing the room with a cool, humid air that stank of dead reptiles.

"I can't take this smell," I declared a half hour later. "Let's open the windows."

So we opened the windows and the odor slowly melted away, along with the hard-won coolness. Again we sweated miserably.

After a few nights of this, even Sylvia was looking forward to a cyclone, anything that would end the sweltering misery. I believed most of the town was of a similar line of thinking. Nothing, I felt, burdens a person's disposition more thoroughly than unrelenting heat and humidity. Vila was generally a friendly town. But now, as people stood fanning themselves in the shade, quietly suffering through the cruel stillness and the enervating stickiness, tempers began to flare, sudden bursts of frustration that broke through the unhappy listlessness.

And then, one morning, Radio Vanuatu announced, in three languages, that the arrival of Cyclone Paula was imminent. All precautions should be made. Those living in low-lying areas should move to higher ground. Homes should be secured, shutters installed. Bulletins would be announced every hour, updating listeners on the cyclone's progress. It would hit that evening.

I couldn't wait.

IT BEGAN, for us, inauspiciously. Attached to the house was a heavy wooden shed where the cyclone shutters were kept. I pried the door open and immediately knew that creepy things lived inside. In the tropics, creepy things can reliably be found in damp, dark places, and the shed was particularly damp and dark, with innumerable nooks and crannies. I startled an impossibly large spider, as big as my hand, and it scurried behind one of the shutters. What else could there be? I wondered. More centipedes? My mind turned to snakes. One of the neighborhood youths had recently caught a six-foot-long Pacific boa constrictor. He was in the habit of walking around with it, dangling it from his arms. I had always given him a wide berth.

I entered the shed and reached for the nearest shutter. It was heavy and ungainly, and as I pulled it free, a centipede ran toward my feet. I shrieked, managing to hit an octave I'd thought I had lost with the onset of puberty.

"What?" Sylvia cried, running out of the house.

I offered a colorful tirade of cuss words in response.

"Okay," Sylvia said. "But what did you see?"

I jiggled the shutter. Out ran the centipede.

"Oh my God," Sylvia gasped. "That's a centipede?"

This time, however, I knew what to do. I went back inside the house and changed into my jeans and work boots. I grabbed a shovel, reentered the shed, and did battle, eventually chopping the centipede into two and then four squirming pieces. *Splat!* it went as I crushed each segment with my boots.

With much fear and trepidation I dragged each of the shutters out, laying them on the ground, where I inspected them closely to see whether there might be another centipede clinging on, hoping to avenge its lost brethren. The first bands of rain had arrived. The clouds above had begun to swirl, and they had taken on a peculiar orange hue. As we affixed the shutters over the windows, the rain steadily increased. We had a steep dirt driveway that sloped toward the house from the road above, and soon water was rushing down it, carving gullies that channeled the water directly to our front door, where it began to pool alarmingly. If I had known that cyclones involved so much work, I reflected, I might not have been so looking forward to experiencing one. Something needed to be done about the water immediately, or we would soon find ourselves flooded. I grabbed the shovel.

Out on the road, Sylvia and I encountered the neighbors across the way. The children were gleefully celebrating the rain. It had begun to truly pour, a copious drenching that laid down thick walls of water. I had seen such rain before, during the brief peak of a Mid-Atlantic summer squall, but I had never witnessed such a sustained downpour, and it only seemed to grow in intensity. The neighbors were laying cinder blocks on top of their corrugated-tin roofs. "If you want to take shelter in our house," I said to one of the mothers, "please don't hesitate to come down."

Looking at our house from the road, I understood why she didn't leap at the offer. Water, of course, is subject to gravity, and our house seemed to possess a considerable gravitational pull. The runoff streamed down the hillside, all of it draining straight down toward the house, where it was rising with startling rapidity. There were two steps leading up to our front door. The water had already engulfed the first step. I brought this to Sylvia's attention. We stood there in the rain, feeling far beyond soaked.

"You know what I'm beginning to worry about?" I said, raising my voice above the thunderous din of rain.

"Mud slides?"

"Exactly."

Somehow, we needed to channel the water so that it cascaded around the house, where it could gush freely down the hillside toward the harbor below us. I no longer cared about flooding. I was worried about the entire house sliding down the hillside once the soil became too soggy to support a foundation. As the afternoon wore on and the rain pelted ever harder with the rising wind I shoveled trenches and troughs—in front of the house, on the slope of the driveway, on the dirt road itself—trying with some desperation to convince the water that it really wanted to go somewhere else. My hands, accustomed as they were to the soft *tap-tap* of the keyboard, were soon bloodied and calloused. The rain was overwhelming, a pounding blizzard of water. Eventually, there was nothing more we could do. I had dug as much as I could. Sylvia had been busy keeping the new trenches free of dirt and debris. Thankfully, most of the water was now flowing alongside the house. What had begun as a steady stream was now a frightful torrent of white water. We stood for a long moment, considering the trenches we had cleared. In a few hours, we had managed to destroy the landscaping around the house.

"The landlord won't be happy," Sylvia said.

"We'll just tell him we had to sacrifice the land to save the land."

Inside the house, we listened to the radio. "Cyclone Paula," said a soothing voice, was "moving to the southeast with sustained winds of 180 kilometers an hour. It can be mapped on the cyclone tracking map in quadrant G-4." The telephone book was handily equipped with a cyclone tracking map, and as the evening progressed we plotted the storm's movements with each weather update. The eye was expected to pass over Efate shortly after 1 A.M. The wind had risen to a strong gale, and we stood on our covered patio watching the palm fronds fold in like blown umbrellas.

As a gloomy, howling darkness descended we attached the last shutter over the glass sliding door leading to the patio. We had now officially battened down the hatches. The wind fetched up alarmingly, and looking through the slats in the shutters, I could see branches and twigs flying through the night. By 11 P.M., the power had been lost. In the darkness, we listened to the shortwave radio. The eye of the storm was now on a direct course for the north part of the island. The house had begun to shudder, buffeted by ferocious winds. I was beginning to worry about the roof. The wind had passed through the howling stage, lingered briefly in screaming mode, and was now hurtling like a rumbling locomotive.

"Isn't this amazing?" I said.

I was somewhere in that sweet spot between wonder and fear. We opened the glass sliding door and peered through the slats.

"All three banana trees are gone," Sylvia noted.

"Papaya trees too," I said. "And look, there goes the gardening shed."

At that instant, before we could stop him, Pip leapt through the slats and vanished into the night.

"Tell me the cat didn't just do that," I said.

"We have to get him!" Sylvia pleaded. "He's just a kitten."

I looked at her. "PIP!" she yelled frantically. "PIP!"

Where had this come from? I wondered as the rain seeped in. At best, Sylvia had always been ambivalent about the cat. She didn't despise it, but as far as I could tell, she had no great affection for it either.

"You have to go find him," she pleaded.

"But there's a cyclone," I observed. "In cyclones, people are supposed to stay inside a shelter. They're not meant to wander about in hundred-mile-per-hour winds looking for lost kittens."

"He's just a kitten," she protested. "Go get him."

"But . . . it's windy."

"PIP!" Sylvia yelled through the slats. "PIP!"

Stupid cat, I thought as I grabbed a flashlight. I left the house through the front door, the only exit left without a shutter, and crept around the side of the house, keeping the walls between me and the full brunt of the storm. Still, the wind and rain were such that I was soon drenched. The trees were bent and anarchic. I reached the small expanse of our backyard, then stuck my hand out and felt the cyclone. The wind nearly popped my arm out of its socket. The rain smacked my hand like pellets. Branches, twigs, and all sorts of indistinguishable projectiles were hurtling through the air. It occurred to me that cyclones are a lot more fun when you're watching them on television. I had moved well beyond awe and was now seized by the grip of fear.

I knew one thing. The cat could have gone in only one direction—with the wind. I shone my flashlight on the bushes lining the fence. "PIP!" I yelled. Stupid cat. "PIP!" I scanned the trees. No, I thought. There's no way he would have made it into a tree. I scanned the bushes again. There he was, huddled like a wet rat in the narrow space between a shrub and the wooden fence. I could see him crying out, but I could hear nothing over the thunderous roar of the cyclone. I turned the flashlight into the wind, searching the sky for sheets of tin and other items capable of inflicting a sudden decapitation. I made a dash for it, leaning my weight into the maelstrom. I was smacked by a thousand leaves. The rain stung. A twig hit me in the back of my head. I grabbed the cat and fought my way through the wind back into the house.

"Pip. There you are," Sylvia cooed, rushing forward and toweling him off.

I stood in the doorway, drenched and panting.

"Um . . . could I have a towel too?"

IN THE MORNING, once the cyclone had been reduced to a gale, we emerged from the house and surveyed the damage. The gardening shed had been lost, along with the fruit trees. Our front yard and the driveway had disappeared under a foot of mud. Everything else, unsurprisingly, was a mess, a jumble of tree limbs, branches, and leaves. But the house still stood. And Pip had remained among the living. Stupid cat.

We walked into town. The permanent structures had withstood the cyclone, though here and there, a roof had been lost. Anything with a thatch roof had to be written off. Most of the smaller fruit trees had been toppled, and a good many of the larger trees had been knocked over too. The whole town seemed to have been inundated with a blizzard of wet leaves. At the harbor, we counted eight yachts sunk, their masts just cresting above the surface. But all in all, Port Vila had escaped the worst a cyclone could offer.

A Chinese shop was, inexplicably, open for business, and we walked in seeking basic provisions. Before the cyclone, Radio Vanuatu had suggested that people stock up on food and water. We'd followed this advice closely and bought a bag of cookies. Now we were in need of both, so we bought a few bottles of water and, as there was nothing else available beyond a few rusty cans of chicken curry, another bag of cookies. Remembering the state of our yard, I also purchased a machete.

"You know what this feels like?" I observed as we headed home. "It feels like a snow day."

And now it was time to do the tropical equivalent of shoveling snow. As a child growing up in Canada I was, of course, very familiar with shoveling snow. But a few hours later, as the machete left my hand, hurtling through the air like a tomahawk when all I had meant to do was hack away at a torn branch, I acknowledged that I was not quite in my milieu here. We spent the day hacking at dangling tree limbs and shoveling mud. Since I was out there trimming, I figured, I might as well prune the hedges, which had grown to such a height as to obscure what there was of our view. There was something vaguely enjoyable about the chore, and the results of my efforts were satisfying. The heat and humidity of the previous days had blown away, and there was a steady cool breeze. I felt like we had survived something, and surviving anything always left me feeling very happy. Everyone we had encountered seemed to be of a similar disposition. Cyclones can kill. It was one thing to know this in a theoretical sort of way. It was something else entirely to actually experience a cyclone and realize that you were just a gust or two away from joining Dorothy in Oz. Not everyone was so lucky, alas. Flooding had taken lives elsewhere in Vanuatu. But we didn't know this then, and like everyone in Port Vila, I felt pleased to just be here, on the island, cleaning up.

It was as I was standing there, enjoying the fruits of my labor, that I felt an astonishingly painful jolt on my foot. The blood suddenly drained from my head. Then I experienced another spasm of pain on my other foot. I looked down and saw a foot-long centipede scampering down the hillside.

It felt like the concentrated effort of a thousand wasps, all plunging their stingers into the same spot. The pain was horrendous. I felt decidedly wobbly.

"Centipede," I cried hoarsely, staggering up toward the house in my flip-flops. I felt cold. My feet throbbed.

"Another one?" Sylvia asked.

My feet were beginning to feel numb, disconnected from the rest of my being. "It bit me," I said, reaching the patio.

Sylvia gasped appreciatively. I felt odd, bloodless. Was this shock?

"Aspirin," I said. "Do we have aspirin?"

"Tylenol," Sylvia said, running inside the house to search through our supply of medicine. I took three tablets. I had no idea whether it would do any good.

"Do you want to go to the hospital?" Sylvia asked.

I considered. Island hospitals were places to be avoided if possible. And the morning after a cyclone, it was likely to be busy anyway. "Let's just see what happens," I wheezed.

The centipede had stung me on the tops of my feet. My left foot swelled to the size of an orange, my right foot to the size of a grapefruit. The skin around the wounds crinkled in a very strange manner, like elephant skin. I could hardly feel my feet. They dangled bizarrely. Well, I thought, what more could nature do?

A WEEK LATER, I found myself hobbling around the house. I had taken an island attitude toward my ailments. I was alive. Why see a doctor? Now and then, I'd pinch the tops of my feet, wondering if I'd ever have feeling again. They were still hideously swollen. It could be worse, I thought. At least I didn't have to wear shoes.

I had noticed that the neighbors had rebuilt their nakamal. Excellent, I thought. Surely, a few bowls of kava would reduce the swelling. If not, I figured, at least I would find a certain equilibrium in the numbness.

"So, tell me what you see," Sylvia asked as I awaited the red light of the nakamal. "One line or two?"

She thrust a thermometer-like contraption in my hands. "Well," I said, "I see two lines, very clearly."

"Do you know what that means?"

"No idea."

"You're going to be a daddy."

CHAPTER 8

In which the author travels to the island of Tanna, where he ascends an active volcano; witnesses the extraordinary Nekowiar ceremony, culminating with the slaughter of two hundred pigs; and meets with villagers deep within the forest who live according to the tenets of kastom, which is another word for naked.

I F THERE IS A STRANGER PLACE TO FIND ONESELF AT FIVE o'clock in the morning than perched atop the narrow rim of an active volcano, I cannot quite imagine what that place might be. But this is where we found ourselves one morning, cautiously peering into the steaming cauldron of Mount Yasur, a provocatively lively volcano on the island of Tanna.

We were playing a little game with Mother Nature. After the excitement of Cyclone Paula, we had asked her, *What else you got?* She responded with Cyclone Sose. Okay, we said, two cyclones within a month is pretty good. What else do you have? She came back with an earthquake. It arrived one afternoon, completely unannounced, which is the thing about earthquakes, their very suddenness. Say what you will about cyclones, but at least they call ahead. We were idling at home when suddenly the house lurched left and then right.

"Whoa," I said.

And then the earth continued to shake and rumble, rising and falling in intensity, for eternal second after eternal second. "Let's get out of here," I said, reaching for Sylvia as the bookcase tottered and the lamp swayed. We dashed outside. The children across the road giggled.

So it wasn't a ten on the Richter scale. But that's what makes earthquakes, in my mind, so terrifying. If I had been told that on Saturday, at precisely 4:47 P.M., there was to be a magnitude 3.8 earthquake, well, I might have grabbed a Tusker, settled into my chair, and enjoyed myself. But earthquakes aren't considerate like that. When the ground begins to shake, you have no idea whether this is going to be just a little tremble, a slight rumbling of the continental plate, or whether this is your own personal end times.

What really got us marveling about Mother Nature, however, was the imminent prospect of parenthood. Technically, I knew where babies came from. Nevertheless, it was impossible not to feel suffused with a sense of cosmic wonderment, knowing that in nine short months, I would be admiring the contents of a baby's diaper. This was life, a life that we had created. And what a miraculous thing that is. Every day our little embryo was sprouting a limb and growing a brain. "According to the book," I said to Sylvia, "our child presently has a tail. Do you think that comes from my side or yours?"

With each passing week, the baby developed eyes and ears, fingers and toes. Time, suddenly, took on a whole new meaning. Babies, we were confidently told by other parents, change your life in ways you cannot even begin to imagine. If you were planning to do anything at all that did not involve a changing table and a diaper bag, now might be a good time to do it. Well, we thought, it might be nice to see a volcano, and since to the best of our knowledge there weren't any volcanoes with stroller paths, we soon found our way to Mount Yasur.

It was the same volcano that had lured Captain Cook to Tanna.

He had noticed its red glow in the night and heard its constant rumbling, and so he brought the *Resolution* toward a small bay on the southeastern side of the island, which he named Port Resolution. There is a small black-sand beach at the mouth of the bay, and Cook soon found its shore occupied by what he estimated to be a thousand armed warriors. If it had been me standing on the quarterdeck, I would have said, "Right, Jenkins. Make a note of it—*Natives hostile.* Now, let's turn this barque around and get out of here." Captain Cook, however, decided to hop in a rowboat and pay the islanders a visit. With a few men, he rowed toward the beach. Feeling that the natives were just a little too close for comfort, he gave an order for a musket to be fired over their heads. Here, in Cook's words, was the response: "In an instant they recovered themselves and began to display their weapons, one fellow shewed us his back side in such a manner that it was not necessary to have an interpreter to explain his meaning."

What this conclusively proves, of course, is that mooning transcends culture. A display of the buttocks speaks a universal language. In the end, Cook was fairly well received on the island, though tolerated might be the more apt description. He tried very hard to be conscientious in naming the island. One of his men, a Mr. Forster, had pointed to the ground, indicating to one of the locals that he'd like to know the name of this place. Tanna, he was told. Tanna it is, then, wrote Captain Cook, filling in his chart, and so to this day the island remains known as Tanna, which means "ground" in the local language.

Captain Cook, however, was prevented from approaching Mount Yasur, which from his description was in a particularly active phase—"The volcano threw up vast quantities of fire and Smoak, the flames were seen to ascend above the hill between us and it, the night before it did the same and made a noise like thunder or the blowing up of mines at every eruption which happened every four or five minutes."

We were more fortunate. Mount Yasur was currently shuttling back and forth between levels 1 and 2 on the four-point scale used by the islanders to describe the volcano's activity. Level 4 is merely an innocuous shorthand for *You're all going to die.* Level 3 says *Those of you on the volcano are going to die,* which was precisely the fate of a Japanese woman and her two guides shortly before our arrival. "We told her it was unsafe," said William, the manager of the village-run guesthouse we were staying at in Port Resolution. "But she wanted to take pictures. No, no, we said. Too dangerous for pictures. But she wouldn't listen to no from the guides. So two boys from the village agreed to take her, and they all die."

"And at what level was the volcano when that happened?" I asked, suddenly sobered by the prospect of standing on its rim.

"It was at level three."

We had arrived at the guesthouse the previous morning. "Just breathe into the paper bag," Sylvia had said onboard the Twin Otter as we were buffeted by crosswinds. The guesthouse was set on a ver-dant bluff overlooking the sky-blue waters of Resolution Bay. Our hut, with walls of pandanus and a roof of thatch, stood just a few yards from a sheer cliff, not a place to amble about in the darkness without a courtesy kerosene lantern. In the mornings, the staff placed a hibiscus flower on the bed, underneath the mosquito net, which we agreed was a classy touch.

On the beach we had noticed steam rising from the tidal pools. Elsewhere, we could see steam rising in irregular bursts from the forest. This was the volcano venting. At a shallow tidal pool, we had come across a family boiling cassava and yams. "Do many people cook their food here?" we had asked. "Yes," replied the father. "Bachelors."

Across the bay rose the small eminence of Cook's Pyramid, a rock from which the captain had sought to calculate where precisely he was on this planet. No doubt he would have recognized the anchorage. A verdant tangle of trees and wildflowers scaled the cliffs rising from the bay. A villager paddled his outrigger canoe across the emerald waters, periodically slapping his paddle on the water's surface, beckoning the dugong, or sea cow, that lived there.

"Do you see it?" Sylvia asked later from our cliff-top perch. It was a nine-foot-long dugong that had popped its head up for a look around. No doubt, he was as perturbed by the sight as we were, and I daresay Captain Cook would have been, for an armada of French yachts had settled in the bay. They were, as we soon learned, from New Caledonia, participating in the annual sailing race from Nouméa to Port Vila. Now, typically, I don't like to make grand generalizations about a people, but I'll make an exception for the French colonists living in New Caledonia. They are pushy, rude, impertinent, and obnoxious, all the attributes generally attributed to Americans traveling abroad. We first encountered them in the village of Yakuveran, just beyond Port Resolution. I was playing soccer with the village youths, feeling profoundly humbled at every turn as these barefoot boys demonstrated why Vanuatu was the preeminent soccer power in the Pacific, when suddenly the colonists arrived, loudly streaming across the village clearing where we were playing. "France against Vanuatu!" yelled one man boozily in French, picking up the ball midgame. Half of us left the field. Most of the new arrivals were well on their way to drunkenness. As they played, their women and children were on the sidelines yelling, "Allez, allez. Vive la France!" Where once the village youths were playing with a dazzling ferocity, they had now lowered their game to accommodate the sloppiness of the French.

"Why are they letting the French win?" I asked the teenage boy next to me.

"Because it will make them happy," he said.

Taking wary note of the yachts, we made arrangements to ascend the volcano late in the afternoon. William had a pickup truck waiting for us. "You stay until after dusk," he said, "and see the magma in the darkness." When we arrived to meet our guides, however, we discovered that the truck had been commandeered by the French. "I am very sorry," William said, meaning it. "What can I do? Is it okay if you go in the morning before dawn?" No problem, we said as the truck heaved off, laden to the hilt with colonists. They returned some hours later, drenched through from a sudden downpour, which amused us immensely.

At dinner that evening, we shared a long table with the colonists. "I am a veteran of the war in Chad," said a burly Frenchman. He had been hitting on Sylvia throughout the meal in that slurpy manner some middle-aged men have whenever they find themselves in the presence of a blond. We asked him about New Caledonia. We had spent the New Year's holiday in Nouméa, the capital, and had found it bizarre, a sunny police state where the French frolic while the Kanaks, the indigenous Melanesians, are sent deep into the mines.

"C'est paradis," he said. Like most of them, he spoke only French.

"Perhaps you could help us understand something," I said. "Why are you there? Or rather, why are the French still in New Caledonia? The nickel that you mine does not come anywhere close to matching the subsidies that the French government sends you each year. And as far as I can tell, France has no particular strategic interests in the region."

"It is our patrimony," he said. "After Algeria, we said never again." The others nodded. "New Caledonia was France yesterday. It is France today. And it will be France tomorrow."

Vive la France!

They're mad, I tell you. But the answer pleased me, for now I felt free to truly despise them, a feeling that peaked sometime after midnight as we lay awake, groaning to yet another loud, drunken rendition of "La Marseillaise." I mean, really now. Who on earth stays up deep into the night singing the national anthem of a faraway motherland? They're nuts, and I had for them nothing but ill will. Okay. Enough. But the next time Germany invades . . . Okay, I'll stop now . . . well, it's not going to be me saving their ass.

MOUNT YASUR is often described as the world's most accessible volcano. It rises to no great height, a mere one thousand feet, and a four-wheel-drive vehicle can easily deposit you within three hundred feet of the summit. It will tolerate, now and then, the presence of drunken paleo-nationalist Frenchmen. It even lent its name to one of the tribes on *Survivor: Vanuatu,* the television game show, which was filmed on the island of Efate, on a beach a short distance from the comforts of Port Vila. These facts may lull some—until, that is, they find themselves in Yasur's fiery presence. The landscape of Tanna is flamboyantly green, a veritable Eden, and so to come across the Ash Plain, a grim, forbidding, lifeless savannah of desolation, is to be reminded that Mount Yasur is very much alive. Indeed, the volcano has been continuously active, rumbling and emitting great torrents of magma and lava bombs, for more than eight hundred years. Near the base stands Lake Isiwi, a large, poisonous pond containing scores of uprooted trees, deposited there by cyclones. Already, here, one can inhale the sulfur and feel the trembling of the ground whenever Mount Yasur flares. Ash is continuously expelled from the crater, and as these plumes of dirt rise and billow from the summit, it occurs to you that standing on the rim is perhaps not the most reasonable or prudent thing to do.

It took a while for this last thought to find us. When we awoke, in darkness, to the insistent *tap-tap* of William knocking on our hut, my first thought, as I remembered why we had slept so little, was to wonder whether I could hit the yachts anchored in the bay below us with a few well-aimed rocks. The lights on their boats presented an appealing target. And then I felt an overwhelming need for coffee.

"No coffee," William declared. "The guides are here. Here are your flashlights."

We stumbled onward, following the glare of the flashlights. A light drizzle fell. Our guides were Simi and Joseph, two men from a nearby village, one of several that claimed to be the traditional landowners of Mount Yasur. Sylvia joined Joseph in the cab of the truck, and I hopped in the back with Simi. I cannot say I had any great enthusiasm for sitting on the cold, wet metal rail of a pickup truck. It was 4 A.M. I was shivering. It is rare to feel cold in the South Pacific, but that is the state in which I found myself. We gingerly made our way toward the volcano, following a muddy trail illuminated by the truck's headlights. We crossed the barren Ash Plain. Above, I could see the red blaze of Mount Yasur reflecting off wet clouds that swirled low above its rim. The air had begun to smell strongly of sulfur, like a million extinguished matches. The truck slowed, and Simi jumped down to unlock a gate that crossed the path leading up toward the rim.

Mount Yasur was the most famous landmark in Vanuatu, and the few visitors who traveled to Tanna paid hefty sums for the privilege of ascending its peak. Since my trip to Malekula, I had come to appreciate outer-island tourism, such as it is, in Vanuatu. The islands are hard to get to. They lack roads, electricity, running water, and pretty much everything else that all but your more intrepid traveler yearns for on a vacation. There is no threat of a Hilton resort opening up on an outer island anytime soon. And yet, for the privilege of traipsing about the mud on an island infested with malaria, sleeping in primitive shelters lacking in amenities, and dining on food that is, at best, a nutritional chore to be endured, visitors find themselves hemorrhaging money. Want to see a kastom dance? 2,000 vatu. See a waterfall? 1,500 vatu. Climb a volcano? 5,000 vatu. See a circumcision ceremony? 10,000 vatu. In the end, it would be much cheaper to take the package deal to Bora-Bora. But what I liked about visiting the outer islands of Vanuatu was that not a dime of what one spends leaves the island. Everything goes to the villages, and you feel good knowing that you have done nothing to contribute to the delinquency of Paris Hilton.

The truck began its ascent, following a steep path that climbed a ridge. Simi seemed to be perking up. So far, both of us had spent the trip silently curled deep within ourselves, seeking to fend off the wet cold.

"Have you been to the volcano many times now?" I asked him.

"Yes," he said, "many times." He paused for a moment. "But it is not the kastom to go to the volcano."

"In kastom times, people didn't go to the top of the volcano?"

"No. It was taboo."

Indeed, Cook had tried to march toward Mount Yasur on his own. Fortunately for him, he soon discovered that without a guide the trek would prove to be too daunting, and he turned around, just in time to encounter thirty armed warriors who had been dispatched to prevent him from approaching the volcano.

"So what's it like up there?" I ventured.

"You must pay attention," Simi said. "When the magma comes up over the rim, do not run."

"Do not run?"

"No, do not run. You must stop and watch where it goes, and then you can get out of the way."

I was certainly awake now.

"Yasur is very unpredictable," Simi continued. "It can change at any time. It is very dangerous."

"Do you like going to Yasur?"

"No. I do not like it."

Joseph stopped the truck. We had arrived. Immediately, we heard the whooshing, the volcano breathing. It sounded like a sloshing ocean encased within a chamber of stone. The putrid smell of sulfur was overwhelming. With unsettling frequency there were loud blasts, explosions. The drizzle had lifted, and as we alighted from the truck, the ground felt strangely warm under our feet.

Sylvia and I exchanged glances. We were not in our element here. This was not a place for humans. Indeed, this was not a place for life. Even in the darkness, we could sense the desolation.

"Remember," Joseph said. "When you see the magma come up over the rim, do not run. You must watch where it falls."

With our flashlights on we followed a narrow trail to the summit, weaving around boulders and steam vents. *Whoosh.* We could hear fiery blasts. It seemed evident to us why this volcano was taboo. Something else lived here, something fearsome and terrifying. As we crested the rim we were greeted with a swirling cauldron of steam radiating an ethereal red. A gray dawn began to emerge. The crater was nearly a thousand feet across, and seeing these hazy red clouds of steam whirling below was like viewing an immense witches' brew.

"Be careful," Simi cautioned. "It is very steep."

Only a few steps in front of us, the ridge plummeted three hundred feet. We stood as close to the edge as we dared. The ground around us trembled and shook. With each blast, smoke ascended.

Magma and lava bombs exploded like firecrackers, arcing across the expanse of the crater, just below the rim. There were three open vents spewing and foaming with magma. As the sky grew lighter the steam caused by the drizzle earlier began to dissipate. We began to walk around the rim, stupefied by the spectacle.

"Do not go too far," Joseph warned us. "This is the highest point. There," he said pointing to his right, "is lower. More chance of magma going over the rim."

The sun rose, and the contrast between the expanse of the volcano and the rest of Tanna was stark. The island was exuberantly alive. We could see the lofty eminences of Mount Tukosmera and Mount Melen, both rising above three thousand feet, with verdant, green ridges, an endless canopy of trees that extended in every direction toward the ocean. But around us, and stretching for a long distance, was nothing but a barren wasteland, populated by car-sized boulders and gray ash.

"Let's go back to the higher ridge," Sylvia said. We had wandered a ways around the crater, utterly transfixed by the volcano. Now we noticed that Joseph and Simi had remained on the highest point of the rim, where they crouched down, with one eye on the cauldron and one on us.

"Well, that ought to tell us something," I said.

The volcano wheezed and trembled. The blasts seemed to shake even the air. We walked back toward where Joseph and Simi stood. Suddenly, the volcano inhaled, a loud, stretched-out *wheesh*. Time seemed to stop. There was a long, painfully long silence.

The blast brought us to the ground. "Watch where it goes!" I yelled. A long inferno of magma and a cascade of lava bombs stretched high above the rim, up, up it went. The noise was deafening, an ear-puncturing explosion. Black smoke plumed in the crater. We were on our feet now.

"It's coming down," Sylvia shouted.

The magma fell back to earth, swallowed by the cauldron. Briskly, we made our way back to Joseph and Simi.

"Thanks so much," I said as a cloud of ash swirled around us. "We'd like to go down now, please."

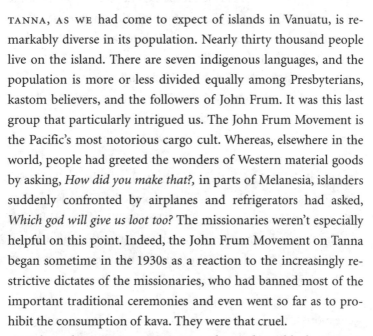

TANNA, AS WE had come to expect of islands in Vanuatu, is remarkably diverse in its population. Nearly thirty thousand people live on the island. There are seven indigenous languages, and the population is more or less divided equally among Presbyterians, kastom believers, and the followers of John Frum. It was this last group that particularly intrigued us. The John Frum Movement is the Pacific's most notorious cargo cult. Whereas, elsewhere in the world, people had greeted the wonders of Western material goods by asking, *How did you make that?,* in parts of Melanesia, islanders suddenly confronted by airplanes and refrigerators had asked, *Which god will give us loot too?* The missionaries weren't especially helpful on this point. Indeed, the John Frum Movement on Tanna began sometime in the 1930s as a reaction to the increasingly restrictive dictates of the missionaries, who had banned most of the important traditional ceremonies and even went so far as to prohibit the consumption of kava. They were that cruel.

A legend arose—its origins are unclear—that told of a mysterious white man who called himself John Frum. He told the islanders to ignore the missionaries and said that if they resumed the old ways and danced and enjoyed kava, he would return one day bearing Western goods, or cargo. For many, this seemed sensible, and they abandoned the churches, took their children out of the mission schools, and set up new villages, where every Friday they danced until dawn. Most unusual for Vanuatu, the women too were encouraged to drink kava.

In the 1940s, the arrival of World War II convinced the followers of John Frum of the righteousness of their cause. Vanuatu, and particularly the island of Santo, was an enormous staging area for the war in the Pacific. Tens of thousands of soldiers passed through the islands, including James Michener, who subsequently based his book *Tales of the South Pacific* on his experiences in Vanuatu. The John Frum followers on Tanna took particular interest in the African American soldiers. It was obvious to them that these black soldiers were originally from Tanna, and that they were fighting for John Frum and the liberation of their island. These soldiers, to their eyes, moved so easily among the white men, whereas they had been accustomed to a rigid hierarchy in which white missionaries and planters ruled. And, of course, there was the cargo, an endless supply of jeeps, planes, iceboxes, radios, and tinned food.

After the war, the followers of John Frum constructed airstrips of their own, clearing the bush in an effort to lure John Frum back to Tanna with his promised riches. They built wooden replicas of the guns they had seen and marched in formation through their village clearings. They danced through the night every Friday and drank prodigious amounts of kava. When John Frum still didn't return with his promised cargo, the believers shrugged and danced some more. Christians, they sagely observed, have been waiting two thousand years for Christ to return.

Today, in the village of Sulphur Bay, in the shadow of Mount Yasur, two flagpoles erected by followers of John Frum continue to fly the baby-blue flag of the U.S. Navy and the Stars and Stripes. This, Sylvia and I agreed, was one of the stranger sights we had encountered in the South Pacific. Almost as an afterthought, another pole carried the national flag of Vanuatu, hoisted grudgingly to appease the government, which periodically clashed with the John Frum Movement over its refusal to pay taxes to the state.

The village was constructed with almost geometric precision, like a barracks, with traditional homes arranged around a grassy ceremonial square. Ponderous waves broke heavily on the beach. Above loomed Mount Yasur, belching ash. It seemed a desolate place. We arrived with William in the afternoon, following our Yasur climb, and we waited as the villagers sat in the shade offered by two great trees. A heated argument of some sort was under way, with one elderly man in a sarong pointing a knobby cane at another elder, seated on an enormous tree root.

Eventually, the elder with the cane made his way toward us. "This is Chief Fred," said William. Chief Fred greeted us warmly. "You are from America?" he asked through William, who acted as a translator.

Yes, we said, we are.

"I have been to America," he said enthusiastically. "I have been to San Francisco, Denver, Houston, New York, and Washington, D.C. I am the Big Man in Sulphur Bay, and I went to meet your Big Men in America."

"And did you meet our Big Men?" I asked.

"Yes. We talked about important things. They asked about Sulphur Bay."

"And what did you tell them."

"That Sulphur Bay is an ally of America."

"Well, I'm sure they were very pleased to hear it."

Sylvia asked, "Did you find traveling to America expensive?"

"Yes," Chief Fred admitted. "It was very expensive. The people worked very hard to send their Big Man to America."

He beckoned us toward the John Frum church, which looked like the other homes but had in its center a red wooden cross.

"I will tell you something," Chief Fred said. "Jesus was from Tanna."

"Ah . . . ," we said. Who knew?

"He was crucified on this cross," he said.

"This one?" I said. Well, I thought, pondering the cross, Jesus must have been a dwarf. The cross was about four feet high and had the symmetry of the cross used by army medics to distinguish themselves from regular soldiers.

"Bethlehem," continued Chief Fred, "was there on the hill, above the village. The River Jordan was Lake Isiwi."

This was all news to us—not simply the fact that we were apparently in the Holy Land but that the followers of John Frum had anything to do with Christianity.

"But," said Chief Fred, "we lost this knowledge. It was only when the missionaries came with the Bible that we learned our history."

"But how did the missionaries learn about Jesus of Tanna?" I asked.

"Jesus flew from Tanna to the land of white man on top of a rainbow."

This was not a point we could argue. And the fact that Jesus was from Tanna . . . well, there are many Americans who believe that God is an American. What was odd about this, however, was that it seemed to refute all that we had heard and read about the John Frum Movement.

"What about John Frum?" Sylvia asked.

"He was a prophet."

"And do you dance on Friday nights?" I inquired.

"Yes, all through the night."

"And do the women drink kava?"

"Yes, women drink the kava."

Thank goodness for that. But still, we found what he had said rather odd. What we didn't know at the time was that the John Frum Movement was on the cusp of a schism. Chief Fred had become, in his own way, a Christian. Another chief, Chief Isaac, accused Chief Fred of heresy. Each had his followers, and soon tensions rose. Not long after we left, Chief Isaac and his followers, the true believers of John Frum, were compelled to leave Sulphur Bay. They created a new John Frum village closer to the volcano. And then the two factions began to fight each other with axes and knives, fists and arrows. Police were flown in from Port Vila. War in Vanuatu, whether between tribes or among religions, remains a serious business on the islands. The future began to look bleak for the John Frum Movement.

On that day, however, we had no intimation of what was to follow. Instead, as we rolled over the Ash Plain, under the simmering volcano, back toward Port Resolution, we and William spent the ride trying to figure out a point Chief Fred had missed: Where was Jerusalem?

ONE MORNING ON TANNA, we found ourselves in Yakel, a kastom village in the interior of the island, watching several men wearing nothing more than a namba shuffle and hop, performing what was allegedly an important traditional dance. Yakel is indeed a kastom village—"a glimpse into the Stone Age," as one enthusiastic visitor had put it. We had been shown where boys were sequestered after their circumcisions. On Malekula it had been a longhouse. In Yakel, it was a treehouse. The villagers' cyclone shelters were located deep within the roots of massive banyan trees. The homes were rudimentary lean-tos, as likely to be inhabited by piglets as by children. The village itself was a muddy enclave hidden in the depths of the forest.

And yet Yakel accepted visitors. Indeed, when we arrived at a trailhead near the village, we were obliged to bang on the tam-tam. I wasn't sure why. To give them a chance to get decent? But no—what the tam-tam said to the village of Yakel was that it was time to get ready. It was showtime. The dance area was a lofty plateau with a glorious view of Mount Yasur huffing and puffing in the distance. But as we watched the leaping buttocks and the recoiling testicles, it was hard to feel as if we were participating in anything other than a peculiar peep show.

"You may take the pictures here," our guide said.

A thousand pictures must have been snapped over the years of the half-naked savages, dancing with their spears, framed by the smoking eminence of Mount Yasur. "And they were cannibals too," one can imagine a colonist from New Caledonia saying with a smirk.

Indeed, they were. It was one of the first things the islanders had asked Captain Cook: *Do you eat people too?*

Now, though, the village had the air of spectacle about it. *Yes, we wear no clothes. Yes, we believe in spirits—1,000 vatu, please.* It wasn't the villagers I reproached for this but us, the visitors, the voyeurs. I felt awkward being in Yakel. Whenever a visitor arrived, the villagers stopped what they were doing and did a little dance—*You can see their balls! The women don't cover their breasts!*—and you got the sense that now that you had been divested of your vatu, they'd prefer that you just shuffle along.

On the morning we visited, however, only a handful of men and women were present in the village, tending to the business of hopping around for travelers.

"Where are the children?" I asked our guide. "Where are the other people?"

"They are at the Nekowiar."

"The Nekowiar? There's a Nekowiar this year?"

What luck, we thought. A Nekowiar—an elaborate three-day alliance-making ceremony between two villages—occurs only every three or four years. We had heard rumors in Vila that there was to be one this year. The exact date was always uncertain. The Nekowiar was, we were told, Vanuatu's grandest bacchanal, and on our return to Port Resolution, we hastily made arrangements with William to move to the other side of the island, near the village of Yaohnanen, deep in the hills, which was hosting the Nekowiar.

"Welcome," said the chief of Yaohnanen when we arrived the following day, muddy and steaming with sweat from the climb up to the village. We had gone as far as we could in the back of a pickup truck until the wheels spun out in the mud. From there, it was another mile of trekking, and we joined hundreds of Ni-Vanuatu marching up the hillside like pilgrims, listening to the songs, the energy emanating from somewhere deeper in the forest. As we neared the village clearing we passed hundreds of snorting and braying pigs enclosed in bamboo pens. These hirsute, tusked swine were soon to be clubbed to death.

"It is still safe," the chief assured us on our arrival. This, of course, suggested that at some point it would also become unsafe. We made a mental note to inquire about this. The chief assigned us a guide, a teenage boy named Kelso. His duty was less to answer our questions than to ensure that we stayed out of the way. As we soon saw, there were more than a thousand people in the tiny village. In the center of the clearing nearly a hundred women, painted and layered with ornaments, swirled in their grass skirts, performing a dance created solely for this Nekowiar.

"This is the *napen-napen*," Kelso informed us. "Today the women dance, tomorrow the men dance the *toka*, and then with first light there will be the *nao*."

We weren't entirely sure what he was talking about, but we paid it no mind and simply watched, fascinated. On the periphery, men taunted the women, who continued to move with a rapturous intensity, ignoring their tormentors. It was fabulous. All my earlier impressions of Ni-Vanuatu dancing were shattered. The women danced with grace and athleticism, perfectly in sync with one another. They also sang in unison.

"The napen-napen," said Kelso, "is about the life of women."

Some of them, we knew, would have their marital fates settled over the coming days. In the past, an alliance between two villages could be forged by exchanging captured men. Of course, the men were meant to be eaten. Now, to deepen the bonds between villages, they agree to share their women. The Nekowiar, however, is also a challenge. Each village is expected to attend the ceremony with a suitably impressive number of pigs. This is a complicated business in Vanuatu, since pigs are what allow men to advance through the grades and hierarchies that color traditional life. No man can possibly have enough pigs to match his obligations, and so he borrows the pigs of others. How well each man manages the debts and obligations involving his need for pigs goes a long way to ensuring whether or not he dies a happy chief. No pigs, no chiefdom. To be invited to participate in the Nekowiar is a huge obligation for villages, because it inevitably divests them of their entire stock of pigs, and it will take them years to recover.

The host village, in order to save face, has to match the number of pigs brought by the village with which they are seeking an alliance. In essence, then, both villages are committing themselves to poverty by agreeing to have a Nekowiar. Then why, one may ask, would two communities agree to do this? It's just a dance, isn't it? Well, it isn't quite just a dance. These are dances infused with magic.

"What kind of magic?" we asked Kelso.

"Beauty magic," he said.

The women had spent months preparing magic lotions and oils. Their faces were painted blood red and crisscrossed with black stripes. The men, Kelso explained, would also be painted for the toka, a celebrated dance for which the men had spent months preparing.

The women before us were still dancing. Indeed, they would dance without pause throughout the night, never flagging.

"How can they keep dancing?" Sylvia asked, raising her voice above the rapturous singing.

"Magic," Kelso explained. "You see, they will not stop until the sun rises tomorrow." Dawn was still a good twelve hours off. "It is because they have the magic."

Well, I certainly couldn't come up with a better explanation. It had been at least four hours since we arrived, and on they danced.

"And you see there?" Kelso pointed to a cluster of elderly men. "Those are the chiefs. They will decide who the women marry."

Clearly, the stakes were high for those participating in a Nekowiar. Before it ended, however, and the new couples settled down to life in a village destined to be impoverished for the foreseeable future, the participants would have the opportunity to experience a night of debauched mayhem. This would follow the dancing of the toka on the second night of the ceremony, and it is what the chief was referring to when he noted that, for the time being, it remained safe. As the men dance the toka, should they encircle a woman—spectators included—they will toss her in the air. A frenzy is reached, and throughout the night, until the first glimmer of dawn, the participants of the Nekowiar are permitted to have sex with anyone they choose. Afterward, they promise that what happens at the Nekowiar stays at the Nekowiar.

We trudged back down the hill, promising to return the following day to witness the dancing of the toka. We hadn't decided yet if we would stay through the night and watch the debauchery. Sylvia, of course, was with child, and a frenzied orgy was probably not the most wholesome environment for expectant mothers. There had been disagreement among the Ni-Vanuatu when we asked whether it was even safe for her to attend. Spectators, we had been told, were fair game for the toka dancers. Alas, in the end, it didn't matter. Disaster struck. In the morning, the sky unleashed a sea of rain. It was unrelenting, and we instead spent the day huddled at the guesthouse. The rain had flooded out a bridge, and until the water receded, we were stuck.

The hours passed. Yaohnanen was unreachable. We scanned the sky, searching for a break in the weather, but it didn't come. We would miss the toka.

The driver of the guesthouse's pickup truck was James, and he was as eager to return to the Nekowiar as we were. "I will check through the night," he said, "and if the bridge is clear, we will go and see the nao." The nao was danced by the men of the host village on the morning after the toka. It was the culmination of the dancing, and we hoped we'd have the chance to see it. Our flight back to Port Vila left later in the morning.

At 4 A.M., we were summoned. We were seeing a lot more of 4 A.M. than we cared for on Tanna, but this time we hopped into the pickup without complaint. The bridge was still flooded, but the water had receded enough to allow us over. James eased the truck through the muddy track that led up to Yaohnanen.

"This is far as we can go," he said as we began to slide backward through the mud. We abandoned the pickup and trudged up through the mire, panting and sweating. Ahead of us, we could hear chanting and stomping. We felt a kinetic energy and fairly bristled in anticipation. Emerging from the forest with the first gray light of

day, we saw hundreds of people running from one end of the clearing to the other, beckoning the dancers of the nao with a rhythmic
cry. The atmosphere was intense, unlike anything I had ever experienced before. The people before us had been awake for three nights
straight, dancing and fornicating, and now this was the climax.

We found Kelso near the pigs. They would soon be slaughtered
for the feast. The young boys were busy chewing and masticating
the kava roots, which had been gathered in enormous piles, and
soon the Nekowiar would end in a kava dream.

"The chief is very angry," Kelso told us. "Someone has used
black magic."

"How does he know that someone used black magic?" Sylvia
asked.

"The rain," Kelso said. "Someone used black magic to cause the
rain."

This struck me as a rather benign manifestation of black magic.
If one's magic was powerful enough to change the weather in the
South Pacific, I think a snowstorm would have made for a more po-
tent demonstration of one's mastery of the dark arts. Causing rain
to fall upon a rain forest during the rainy season was, for me, in any
case, a little unimpressive, nothing more than a black magic card
trick.

"The chief thinks it's one of two people," Kelso added.

"What will happen to the person who caused the rain?" I asked.

"He will be killed," Kelso said.

Kastom, we were learning, was a powerful force on Tanna. Three
hundred men emerged from the forest, led by the chief, who carried
a ten-foot-pole wrapped with feathers. On top were the plumes of a
hawk. The performers, painted and adorned, danced and sang in
unison as the ground trembled beneath them, sweeping everyone
away in an ecstatic collective rapture. It was the most extraordinary

spectacle I had ever witnessed. I had not thought I could be moved by the dancing in Vanuatu. I had always been befuddled by the kastom interpretation of the afterlife: Live a good life, respect the spirits, tend to your pigs, and once you die you will dance into perpetuity. What, I thought, do an endless hokey pokey? What a woeful heaven, I'd imagined. Watching the nao, however, I was soon transported. It was like the bolero of the forest, a rhythmic dance that gathered ever more force as it went through the stages of a man's life. Slowly and surely, the three hundred dancers attained an ecstatic crescendo. This was the Man dance, and watching the dancers, I felt something primal stir. The dancers were farmers and warriors, and while I have never been either, there was something about their interpretation that resonated deep within me—*We are Men. Hear us Roar*—and as we descended the hill to the squeals of pigs being clubbed and drove through the lush hills of Tanna toward the airport, I didn't think anything could possibly end the bliss I felt, not even a Twin Otter to Vila.

CHAPTER 9

In which the author arrives in Fiji and soon finds himself cavorting with prostitutes, which he acknowledges he shouldn't be doing, especially as his wife is in a family way, but seediness, as usual, has a way of finding him.

ONE OF THE EXCITING THINGS ABOUT FINDING YOUR-self pregnant on an island far away from anyplace you've called home is deciding where, exactly, you're going to have the child. Of course, it wasn't me who was pregnant, but I had a strong propri-etary interest in the growing swell of Sylvia's belly. *Tick-tock, tick-tock.* The day was drawing irrecoverably closer, and we had some decisions to make. Sylvia, who was always keen to have as many third-world experiences as she could, decided that childbirth wasn't one of them. Her doctor, a Tuvaluan, had told her, frankly, that if she didn't have to give birth in Vanuatu, then she really shouldn't. The hospital was a grim, dirty place, and if anything out of the ordinary occurred during delivery—and there is always something out of the ordinary—he wouldn't answer for the results. Well, hey, we thought, this is our kid we're talking about. So we consulted the map.

In Vanuatu, most of the Frenchwomen retreated to New Cale-donia to have their babies. I had been nursing a strong antipathy to-ward New Caledonia ever since New Year's, and I had trouble reconciling myself to the idea of having a wee New Caledonian of our own. *The reason he's colicky,* I imagined myself thinking, *is due to the fact that he was born in New Caledonia. They're all whiny over there.* The other foreigners generally returned to their own countries, but we quickly nixed this option. It's funny how long a week can feel when you're visiting the in-laws. Three months, we thought, would probably end in legal proceedings. For a while, we became amenable to the idea of having the child in Australia, despite worries that our son—we sensed he would be a boy—would grow up to have a predilection for wearing short-shorts well into adulthood. But just as Hawaii, Samoa, and New Zealand were all rejected, so too, ultimately, was Australia. They were pit stops. Sylvia didn't want to deliver in a pit stop. She wanted a home.

"My nesting instinct has kicked in," she said, rubbing her swelling belly. "I want"—she thought for a moment—"a rocking chair."

There was only one thing for it: We would move to Fiji a little early. It had always been the plan, and it was just a question of time until FSP International shifted its office to Suva, the capital of Fiji. What's a little political instability, we figured, when we had the opportunity to give our child Fijian citizenship? Later, when he was snowplowing down the ski slope, representing Fiji in the Winter Olympics, he'd be so grateful.

Before moving, Sylvia had to make one last business trip to Sydney, where she'd also receive a checkup. Prenatal care in Vanuatu pretty much stopped at the confirmation of pregnancy. *Yup. You're pregnant. Good luck. Next!* In the meantime, I would be the advance team in Fiji, charged with finding a home for the little fam. Sylvia would meet me a week later in Suva.

"You're sure I can find Vanuatu kava in Fiji?" I asked a friend who had lived there. There was, I knew, plenty of kava in Fiji. The Fijians drank copious amounts of it—at home, at work, at ceremonies—there was hardly any situation in Fiji that did not call for kava. But it was weak kava. Once you've had Vanuatu kava, there's no going back.

"In the covered market in Suva, across from the bus station, on the second floor, there's an Indian named Vijay Patel who sells it in powdered form. Typically, it's from Pentecost, now and then from Tanna. His stall is the third one on the left, two rows in. Tell him I say hey."

"Powdered, not freshly ground?"

"Afraid so. I tried smuggling in some fresh roots, but they were confiscated."

"Tragic. Better have a few shells before I go."

I said good-bye to Sylvia as she boarded the flight to Sydney. We'd meet next in Suva. "Be good," she said. And then I said farewell to Vanuatu. "You are my brothers," I told the group at the nakamal.

Though I would miss the nakamals dearly, I was looking forward to moving to Fiji. When we'd departed the atolls of Kiribati some years earlier, Fiji had been our first stop on the journey home. It seemed huge to us then, profoundly civilized and welcoming, and we enjoyed our stay there immensely. Of course, at the time, we were easily impressed. "Look," I had said to Sylvia in Suva. "An escalator. Do you see? It goes up. And look. That one goes down. Isn't that amazing?" When we discovered that our hotel room on the Coral Coast had both a view of the ocean *and* air conditioning, we were smitten forever.

And, I thought as I boarded an evening flight to Nadi on Air Vanuatu, there won't be any of this pseudo-colonial nonsense in Fiji. No one will call me master in Fiji, I thought confidently. Port Vila had always felt uncomfortably odd, provoking my inner Marxist. I didn't know I had an inner Marxist until I arrived in Vila, and I hoped to leave him behind. Marxists can be so tedious.

It was thus with a happy optimism that I arrived in Fiji. The smell alone was redolent of the Fiji I remembered—the ocean, ripe vegetation, sweat, curry, diesel. There were dozens of taxis lined up outside the airport, and I half-expected a scrum of drivers charging at me, beckoning me with an insistent hail. The Fiji I knew was frothing with hyper-tourism, and noting the scarcity of tourists at the airport, I had prepared myself to be assailed by tour guides and cabdrivers hungry for a customer, any customer. It was with some surprise, then, that I actually had to raise my arm to catch a taxi.

"So how is the tourist business in Fiji?" I asked the young Indian taxi driver as I settled into the front seat, feeling as pleased as pie that I could speak in English and reliably expect to be understood. The radio blared Indian pop music. On the dashboard was a sticker of a dancing blue elephant with an unnatural number of limbs. Nearly half the population of Fiji is of Indian descent.

"Are you a tourist?" he asked.

"Not quite," I said.

"Then we are still waiting for the tourists to come back."

Looking around, I could see why. Nadi was where the international airport was located. The airport gate was heavily guarded by Fijian soldiers carrying M-16s. Not exactly what one wants to see on a honeymoon. We slowly weaved around a series of tire traps. There were eight soldiers, and they were all business, scanning incoming cars with flashlights.

"How is the political situation?" I asked the driver as we merged into traffic.

"The political situation is . . ."

"LOOK OUT!" I yelled. Then the realization hit me. "Heh . . . Sorry. I see you drive on the left side of the road here."

The driver gave me a cautious sidelong glance, no doubt wondering about the stability of his fare. Sensing that I probably wouldn't bite, he continued. "The political situation is very bad," he said animatedly. "Fiji is finished for the Indians. Everybody is trying to leave—Australia, New Zealand, Canada, America. Anywhere. There is no future here."

"That bad?"

"Yes. Fiji is finished."

I hoped it wasn't quite finished yet. After all, we were moving here. Indeed, we would soon have a little Fijian of our own. This would hardly alter the immigration-emigration ratio, of course. I had learned that tens of thousands of Indo-Fijians, most of the educated professional middle class, had already departed for brighter shores. I left the cabdriver to his gloom and checked into the West Motor Inn, one of the innumerable motels lining the road between the airport and Nadi. I was, it appeared, the only customer. I was given a dank room with a balcony, but I could hardly complain, as it also offered air conditioning and cost less than $15 a night. I planned to make the trip to Suva the following day. The capital was on the other side of Viti Levu, Fiji's main island, about five hours from Nadi by bus following the Queen's Road. I could have flown, of course; the flight was a mere half-hour. But if I didn't have to board a Twin Otter, then I wouldn't, particularly after I'd scanned *The Fiji Times,* which had a follow-up article on a recent crash involving an Air Fiji Twin Otter that had flown into a mountain. True, dozens of people died each year on the Queen's Road, but I had survived this long without being rational and saw no reason to change my ways.

So I had an evening to kill. With nothing to do beyond watching the geckoes scamper across the walls of my motel room, I headed out for a walk into town. The length of road between the airport and Nadi, I remembered, was quite likely the most hideous corner of Fiji, a fact I soon confirmed as I stumbled along in the darkness, inches from the *whish* of speeding jalopies. The sight would have been depressing had I not already known that Fiji only gets better from here. It was a long stretch of dilapidated stores, like an American strip mall that hadn't been tended to for thirty years. Most of the businesses were shuttered behind steel bars and wire mesh, locked with chains and padlocks. From the signs, it was apparent that each was Indian owned. Indeed, one would be hard-pressed to even realize that he was presently on an island in the South Pacific and not, as the evidence seemed to indicate, in some provincial backwater in India. The cars raced by, swerving enthusiastically around everything that moved in front of them. They were driven with the casual carelessness that comes easily, I thought, to those sure in the knowledge that they will be reincarnated into perpetuity.

It was humid, and I was beginning to sweat freely. Nadi, it was dawning on me, was much farther from the motel than I had assumed—several miles at least—but I walked on because, well, I didn't have anything better to do. As I neared the town there was a long stretch of bush, a tangle of trees illuminated only by the passing glare of headlights. I proceeded blithely on, but soon I had a sixth sense that something was afoot. I was not, generally, particularly cautious. I rarely thought of myself as a potential victim of criminality. I tended to like people, and this, I thought, was usually enough to disarm all but your most determined mugger. And if that didn't work, I'd scrunch up my face so it suggested that, now and then, when I've had to do it, I've killed. But something was disturbing my inner harmony, and I thought it prudent to turn around and retreat to the light.

Four figures suddenly ran across the road. Men? They were tall, slender, very muscular. They wore pink hot pants. Women? They wore makeup. Cross-dressers? Amazonian queens? They had, evidently, been tailing me for some time.

"You want a blow job, honey?" asked the biggest, a tall, heavily made-up Fijian man in hot pants and heeled sandals, wearing a sleeveless Lycra shirt that emphasized his heaving pecs.

"No. Thanks so much for asking, though."

He approached and locked his arm in mine, guiding me into the trees as his companions followed. "Just give me some."

"No, really, I'll just be on my way."

He was pulling me with greater insistence into the bush. "You want to fuck?" he leered. The others were circling me.

This is not good, I thought. Undoubtedly, I was about to be robbed. Much more troubling—and I mean incomparably more troubling—was the prospect of being sordidly abused by four hulking Fijian cross-dressers. Not my thing at all.

"Get the fuck away from me!" I hissed, yanking my arm away.

He continued to paw at me. "Come on, honey. Give me some." The other three were crowding around.

If they had just asked nicely for my wallet, I might have paused for a moment, considered the odds, and handed it over with barely a whimper, perhaps offering a gentle reminder not to spend it all in one place. They were all well above six feet tall. But there was something about the prospect of being sodomized—I had just arrived, after all—that encouraged me to flee. I dashed for the road and kept running until I reached the relative safety of a streetlamp. I turned to see if they were giving chase, prepared to keep running until my last breath if I had to. I could see them strutting and yelling, swinging their purses. Well, I thought, they're going to have to take their heels off. Unwilling to part with their shoes, they turned and disappeared into the night.

What a lively way to begin a stay in Fiji, I thought as I began to wander back in the direction of the motel, periodically checking behind me, wondering what else might possibly be lurking in the shadows. There was no one else walking alongside the road, and it occurred to me that that ought to tell me something. I flagged a taxi.

"You want a girl?" asked the driver, a thin, unshaven Indo-Fijian man with a cigarette dangling from his lips. On the radio, Bollywood wailed.

For a moment, I thought he might be inquiring about my desired preference in progeny, and I nearly answered that I had no preference, either a boy or a girl would be great, just as long as it's healthy.

"Only Fijian girls here," said the taxi driver as we passed a building that announced it was a Korean restaurant and club. "Fijian girls no good."

"Ah . . . ," I said, realizing that he wasn't talking about sons and daughters. Or at least not mine, in any case. "Thanks, no. I'm fine."

"You like Indian girls? Indian girls are very good. I take you to Dreamland Nightclub. There you meet Indian girls and you choose the one you want."

I was not in the mood for the squalid, and my evening was beginning to take on decidedly squalid overtones. What I really wanted was a beer. "No, thanks. Could you just drop me off in the center of Nadi Town?" I figured I'd walk around a bit and, with any luck, find a quiet bar where I could have a couple of pints of Fiji Bitter and read my book.

"You buy a souvenir here," said the taxi driver, stopping in front of Jack's Handicrafts, "and give them my card. They give you special price."

This was more like the Nadi I remembered, a little outpost of the subcontinent, a place where everything is haggled down from "special price" to "final best price." Curious, I paid the driver and entered Jack's Handicrafts, a well-lit souvenir emporium with twelve sales assistants for every customer. I know because I was the only customer and I counted twelve sales assistants. I picked up a four-pronged "cannibal fork," lingered over the "cannibal clubs" for a moment, and nearly bought an apron that said ISLAND COOKING above a cartoon of a Fijian man in a chef's hat stirring a large pot with two human legs poking out. This would make an excellent Christmas present for several people I knew.

"For you, I'll give a special price," said an Indian sales assistant. The entire staff was Indian. I wondered what the Fijians thought of Indians selling Chinese-made trinkets celebrating Fijian cannibalism.

I declined to make the purchase. In Vanuatu, we had put most of our belongings in a couple of boxes and mailed them to the post office in Suva. Nevertheless, I was still traveling with just about all that I could carry, and the last thing I wanted was more stuff to move. I strolled up the main road, my eyes searching for a sign that said BAR, PUB, BEER, or some derivation promising ale. Instead, nearly every sign read PATEL, SINGH, RAMESH, or some other Indian surname followed by the nature of their wares: KUMAR CLOTHING, SARESH'S HARDWARE. The street was essentially deserted, and I walked up toward the Hindu temple, encountering only a backpacker or two, who appeared as disappointed as I at the apparent lack of bars in downtown Nadi. The town, the guidebooks had said, was the tourist hub of the South Pacific. Someone ought to tell the people of Nadi, I thought.

I turned around, scanning the storefronts again with some peevishness in case I had missed a pub. Soon I found myself walking out of Nadi. I crossed a bridge over a burbling river. As I passed a sign pointing the way to the Sheraton resorts on Denarau Island I made a mental note to send a letter to the Fiji Visitors Bureau. If you want the tourists to come back to this coup-riddled country, I would write, a good place to start would be with a decent bar in the center of town.

"Pssst . . . ," said a voice.

Who was this? I wondered. Not another large cross-dresser, I hoped.

"Psst . . ."

The voice came from the shadows under a looming tree. An Indian girl emerged. She couldn't have been much more than twenty. Three other Indian girls stood behind her.

"Do you want a massage?"

As a matter of fact, I did want a massage. A massage would have been great. I had spent much of the afternoon heaving luggage from one country to another, and I was certainly amenable to a good rubdown. And so it was with some regret that I declined the offer.

"You want to fuck?" she then inquired.

Well, this relationship was certainly moving at a fast clip. "No, thanks. I'll just move along. Good night."

She was very pretty. There are men—lots of them, apparently—who fly thousands of miles for the opportunity to pay a few dollars to sleep with a destitute girl in a third-world country. I couldn't quite see the romance in it, but even if I could, engaging in a commercial transaction of such a nature just wasn't going to happen. I had a vision of standing before my wife, the vessel carrying my child: "Now, honey, don't be like that. The reason I'm taking medication for syphilis . . ."

I chortled at the thought and returned to my quest for beer. I was nearing the dark patch where I'd had my encounter with the cross-dressers. Giving up on Nadi, I hailed another taxi.

"You want . . ."

"No."

I returned to the motel. There was a bar there, I recalled. I settled onto a stool. There was one other patron, an elderly Englishman, who was quietly muttering to himself.

"That's right," he said kindly, turning toward me. "I've been smoking for sixty years now. And I'm in blooming health." He lit a cigarette.

I took a deep breath. I had resolved to quit smoking. There was something about lulling a baby to sleep with one hand while jabbing a lit cigarette with the other that suggested that now might be a good time to quit.

"Nothing wrong with me," he said, dragging deeply. "I enjoy smoking. Always have."

The bartender stood in front of me, waiting for me to order a drink. Behind him was a display of cigarettes. Could I do it? I wondered. Could I sit here and drink beer and not smoke while a deranged Englishman rambles on—and ramble he did—about the joys of smoking? I breathed deeply. I could not, I grimly concluded.

Instead, I soon found myself sitting on the balcony outside my motel room, chewing gum, trying to lose myself in my book. The balcony was on the second story, overlooking a dimly lit side street. A car soon pulled up below me. A Fijian man emerged from the passenger side. He wore an outfit that suggested a devotion to the Jane Fonda line of early-80s aerobic-exercise workout tapes, headband included. This was matched with heels and a purse. He paced back and forth. Another car pulled up, and he hopped in. The car idled. Five minutes later he emerged. As the car sped off he looked up. Seeing me, he sashayed over to just under the balcony. "You want a date, honey?"

No, I didn't want a date. Frankly, I was beginning to feel a little weirded out by Fiji. It's not every day that I'm accosted or solicited by cross-dressers and prostitutes. I had no idea what this portended, but I was looking forward to moving on to Suva. How much more sordid could the capital be?

SUVA IS A CITY that has a way of confounding one's expectations of what a city in the South Pacific ought to be like. Even though I had now lived in Oceania for more than three years and knew how astonishingly varied the islands could be, I could never quite get accustomed to the fact that in Suva, the beating heart of the South Pacific, the sun rarely shone. It's true. Of all the places in the South Pacific available to the English for a regional colonial capital, they chose to place theirs in a rain shadow. I'm not sure why they did this. I had always thought that the weather in Britain, its ceaseless rain and endless gray, was what drove the pursuit of the empire to sunnier climes. And yet, once they reached the South Pacific, what did they do? They placed their administrative capital on the wettest, grayest sliver of island they could find. I don't think the French would have made the same mistake. Looking at the weather map of Fiji, one inevitably saw happy sunshine cascading over all the islands except for that one small corner of Viti Levu occupied by Suva, where invariably rain showers were to be expected into perpetuity.

The other thing that I, at least, had come to expect of towns in the South Pacific was that they were possessed of a calm languorousness, a sleepy essence suggesting that whatever it is that needed to be done now could always be done tomorrow. Suva, however, *bustled*. It was the Midtown of the South Pacific. There were Fijians and Indo-Fijians, of course, but also Polynesians, Micronesians, and other Melanesians from the Solomons, Papua New Guinea, and Vanuatu. There were so many Westerners from Australia, New Zealand, North America, and Europe living there that it remained possible, hypothetically, for them to have affairs without the entire expatriate population knowing about it the following morning. There were Chinese farmers ferrying in produce to the covered market, and a large swath of Victoria Parade, the main road in Suva, had been transformed into a strip of Chinese restaurants and nightclubs catering to the hundreds of Asian fishermen who found themselves in town each day as their catch was weighed in port. The United Nations was represented by approximately 130 separate agencies, doing whatever it is that U.N. agencies do. The Indo-Fijian businessmen had their headquarters in Suva, and many firms from Australia and New Zealand maintained offices in town. The government, of course, had its offices in Suva, and its officials could be seen conducting business wearing *sulus,* the gabardine skirts that only Fijian men can wear with aplomb. The main campus of the University of the South Pacific too was located in Suva—a disappointment, no doubt, to the three or four American students who enrolled there each year, thinking they'd signed on for four years of surfing bliss, and discovered too late that the nearest beach was nearly an hour's drive away.

Standing at the bus station, surrounded by dozens of windowless buses belching thick black clouds of smoke, I found myself feeling bewildered and confused. The bus trip had been exciting as the driver careened around blind corners at one hundred miles per hour, tipping us onto two wheels, only to suddenly swerve to miss a cow idling on the road or screech to a halt in front of one of the half-dozen police checkpoints that had been set up on the Queen's Road. Minibus drivers in Fiji tended to be ex-convicts, not the most risk-averse segment of the population. There was hardly any traffic on the road, and what there was of it, the minibus driver did his best to hit. The closer we got to Suva, the more lush the landscape became. On the western side of Viti Levu, the dry side of the island, fields of sugarcane swayed with the breeze over undulating hills. It was a near-treeless expanse, populated by small Indian bungalows, the homes of the farmers who leased the land from Fijian landowners. On the eastern coast, however, a verdant jungle toppled over steep, cascading hills, a primordial wilderness that rolled on to the edge of Suva.

The capital of Fiji is not the sort of city that goes out of its way to make a good first impression. WELCOME TO SUVA said the sign beside an enormous mountain of garbage, a heaving mound of trash that emptied into Suva Harbor. This would be the town dump. Well, it can only get better from here, you think. A moment later we slowed for a road-improvement project that passed through a flooded cemetery. Construction crews were busy widening the road. I suppose the plan was to just pretend that there weren't any dead bodies. A road grader would smooth dirt until a grave got in the way. Then the road would be graded again from the other side. A moment later, the bus brought us alongside what seemed like a caricature of the grimmest prison you could imagine. Think of where the pasha of Yemen in the thirteenth century would throw those who displeased him, and you might be able to envision Suva Prison, a foreboding, ancient, thick-walled edifice from which you could almost hear the howls of prisoners chained to the walls.

Suva, clearly, was not the South Pacific found in brochures. I made my way to the Peninsula Hotel and was surprised to find that I had checked into what appeared to be, in almost every detail, my college dorm room in Boston. It had the same institutional white cinder-block walls, the same neutral furniture bolted into the floor, and I half-expected to find a keg hidden in the shower. Darkness had descended, and I started down the hill toward town, hoping to find the Hare Krishna Restaurant I had patronized on my visit three years earlier. Walking, I discovered that Fijian towns all seemed to have one thing in common. Typically, on islands in the South Pacific, women tended to give me a curious glance, as they might a straying goat, and then return to their activities. In Suva, however, as in Nadi, I couldn't walk five yards without a woman offering a *pssst* here and a *pssst* there, all promising something carnal and illicit. Walking past a bus stop where a dozen Fijian girls idled, I felt like a rock star. Girls threw their bodies at me. Possibly they thought

I was immensely good looking. Or possibly not. I did discover, however, that if you want to make prostitutes laugh, just mention that you're declining their very generous offer on the grounds that you're married.

After satisfying a hankering for Samosas, I strolled along Victoria Parade. Here at last were a goodly number of bars. Fiji, alas, did not have nakamals. Choosing at random, I walked into a bar calling itself Signals. It was loud and dark, and I stumbled toward the bar, sensing people around me but not really seeing them. It was only after a bottle of Fiji Bitter had been set down before me that my eyes began to grow accustomed to the lack of light. I looked at the booths, scanned the dance floor, glanced at the other patrons loitering at the bar, and came to the inescapable conclusion that I was presently in a Chinese brothel.

"WHERE YOU FROM?" asked an Asian woman, yelling above the throbbing music as she settled onto the stool next to mine.

"VANUATU," I said, to be difficult.

"WHERE?"

"VANUATU."

"WHERE'S THAT?"

"NEXT TO FIJI."

I strummed my fingers on the bar. All the women in the bar were Asian, as were most of the men. I guessed they were Chinese fishermen. They had an air of hard living about them.

"YOU WANT TO DANCE?"

A potbellied Westerner was on the dance floor, flailing about, surrounded by a half-dozen Chinese girls oozing boredom. It would take many, many beers before I'd even consider joining them.

"YOU WANT GOOD TIME?"

Her English was halting, and I sensed that what she did speak had been learned from watching Vietnam War movies. Before she had a chance to inform me that she'd love me for a long time, however, I asked her where she was from.

"I from China."

"Whereabouts?"

"Gwaidongha."

"Where?"

"Xiangoyzh."

I couldn't say I had heard of it.

"You know where North Korea is? On the border."

A long way from home, I thought. I asked where the other girls were from.

"All from same place."

"And have you been here long?"

"Seven months," she said. "I have a one-year work permit."

What a considerate government, I thought.

"So what you say? You want good time?"

I didn't want a good time. After twenty-four hours in Fiji, what I really wanted was a shower.

CHAPTER 10

In which the author embraces Fijian history and culture, particularly the Fijian national rugby team, and discovers rugby to be very exciting, uplifting even, as he finds that when the national team plays, for an hour or two at least, Fiji is harmonious.

I F THERE IS ONE MUSEUM THAT MUSEUM DIRECTORS FROM around the world should be obliged to visit, it is the Fiji Museum in Suva. It is exactly what a national museum ought to be. Generally, when I am abroad, I no longer visit these places. Too often, I have been awakened with a start by a concerned security guard insistently poking at my slumbering form, trying to rouse me from the spot where I have wilted in boredom in front of a display of a walking stick, circa 1815. Stepping into the Fiji Museum, however, I knew immediately that I was going to like it.

Sylvia had finally arrived in Suva, and we were still getting to know the city. On that day, we had had no intention of going to the museum. But, as happened with some regularity in Suva, we found ourselves caught in a sudden downpour, and we scampered toward the nearest shelter, which happened to be the museum. For a repository of a country's history, it is rather small and compact, which immediately left me feeling well disposed toward it. There is something about standing in front of a monumental museum, such as the Louvre, that instantly leaves me with wobbly legs. "Okay, we've seen that pyramid thing in the courtyard. Can we go now?" Three hours later, I'd find myself trailing puddles of drool until, finally, in front of a glass display case containing a gilded cane, Louis XIV, circa 1770, I'd collapse and fall asleep.

Stepping up to the Fiji Museum, we noticed a sign on the wall informing us that the museum had been officially opened in 1999 by the governor-general of New Zealand, a Sir Michael Hardie Boys. This was like being told that the Louvre had been opened by Tintin. Inside, the exhibition room was dominated by an enormous *drua*, a wooden catamaran used on the open ocean by the Fijians of yore. I stood admiring the boat for a while, until Sylvia brought to my attention a curious display case. It contained a Bible said to be the ordination Bible used by Reverend Thomas Baker, a Methodist missionary who arrived in Fiji in the 1860s with the aim of converting the tribes living in Viti Levu's remote Nausori highlands. Well, ho-hum, I thought. What's next, his school report card? Not quite. Instead, there was a small wooden bowl—*Dish in which some of Mr. Baker's flesh was presented to one of the highland chiefs,* read the description. I had never regarded a wooden bowl in a museum with quite the same level of fascination as I did this one. Alongside it was the wooden fork used for eating Mr. Baker's flesh. And the most compelling item, the remains of Mr. Baker's shoe. This was history come alive, I thought. It appeared that the Reverend Baker had made a fatal faux pas. Perturbed to find that the highland chief had borrowed his comb, Baker snatched it back. Alas for him, the chief was storing the comb in his hair, and in Fijian culture, yanking something out of a chief's hair is a big no-no. Soon all that remained of the Reverend Baker was the sole of his boot.

It didn't take much, I learned, to get yourself killed in Fiji. While the cannibalism in Vanuatu had left me bewildered, the scale of the bloodshed that colored traditional life in Fiji left me agape with horror. Consider, for instance, the construction of a temple honoring one of the gods. Human sacrifices were called for when the foundation posts were cut. More were needed when the posts were raised. Still more bodies were required once the rafters had been tied together. Naturally, one could hardly call the temple complete without another batch of dead bodies. And still more sacrifices were needed when the god's favorite shells were hung. Well, that's interesting, you think. The temple came complete with a full cemetery. But there was no cemetery. The Fijians had another way of disposing of the bodies. They ate them.

Even the language suggested a frightful existence. *Coco,* or grass, referred to the chief's wives, who had been strangled so that they could follow their husband into the afterlife. *Lago,* or logs, were the men who had been killed so they could be used as rollers for the launching of war canoes. *Manumanu-ni-laca,* birds-of-the-sail, were dead children from an enemy's village who had been strung up on the yardarms of a war canoe. This was a culture devoted to killing, and when there wasn't an enemy around to meet their needs, chiefs took to killing the commoners among them.

Generally, when it came to missionaries, I rooted for the home team. "My god is better than your god" always struck me as an argument that was just a trifle presumptuous. What if the missionaries were wrong? What if the divine creator was actually Isis, the goddess of fertility? She'd be pissed, wouldn't she? Nevertheless, after just a brief exploration of Fijian history, I couldn't help but cheer for the Methodists.

The people of Nubutautau, the village where the Reverend Baker was consumed, had begun to feel a little bad about the matter. Indeed, ever since their ancestors ate the reverend, they felt that their village had been plagued with bad luck. To make amends, they'd presented a *tabua,* or whale's tooth, to the Methodist Church.

If you really want to say you're sorry in Fiji, do it with a whale's tooth. Indeed, Sitiveni Rabuka, the army colonel who led Fiji's first coup in 1987, had sent a whale's tooth to Queen Elizabeth, the titular head of Fiji, demonstrating that he was very sorry for upsetting her with the coup, wouldn't do it again, promise, now can we please rejoin the Commonwealth? The whale's tooth that Nubutautau gave to the Methodist Church was displayed in the museum together with a photo of the Reverend Baker's great-grandniece, who had traveled to the village to participate in a forgiveness ceremony. Makes you feel all soft and fuzzy inside, doesn't it?

Now why, I wondered, couldn't other national museums be like this one? Not only did the Fiji Museum contain compelling artifacts like the remains of the Reverend Baker's boot, but it also displayed random curios for no other reason than the simple fact that they happened to be in Fiji—things like the rudder of the *Bounty*. The mutiny had nothing to do with Fiji, though Captain Bligh and the loyalists did sail through the islands on their way to Java, but Bligh wisely declined to make landfall in Fiji lest the sole of his shoe also one day join the museum's collection. Even the walking sticks were fascinating to behold. They were made of human bones, circa 1850. See what I mean? It's fun for the whole family.

Once the shower had passed, we started walking toward the center of Suva. With Sylvia beside me, the *psst*s had stopped, though here and there, I'd receive a friendly hello from the ladies of the night.

"And who was that?" Sylvia asked.

"That was Ramona."

"And did you meet many women during your week alone in Suva?"

"Many women. They're very friendly in Suva. But Ramona's not actually a woman."

"Ramona's not a woman?"

"Fooled me too."

It was a strange time to be in Suva. The number of women—and men—who had turned to prostitution attested to how convulsive the coup had been for people in Fiji. It had been a particularly traumatic experience for those in Suva. The front man had been George Speight, a ne'er-do-well son of a politician. He and his co-conspirators had stormed the parliament and taken much of the government hostage, including Prime Minister Mahendra Chaudhry. Speight said that he was acting in the name of indigenous Fijians and promptly declared that, henceforth, all power resided with him. Within hours, thousands of Fijian sympathizers had surrounded the parliament. They encamped there, and soon mob rule descended on Suva. Hundreds of Fijian toughs laid waste to the city. The duty-free shops burned. The cafés were torched. An army of looters carted off stashes of televisions and jewelry, food and perfume. The police disappeared, ceding the city, the pride of English rule in the Pacific, to anarchy.

Elsewhere in the country, long-simmering grievances between indigenous Fijians and Indians had erupted into rolling spasms of violence and intimidation. Between 1879 and 1916, more than sixty thousand Indians had arrived in Fiji as indentured laborers, recruited or tricked into coming by the British, who needed cheap labor to work on the sugar plantations. Most of their descendants still earned their living cutting sugarcane, leasing the land from the Fijians who own 87 percent of all the land in Fiji. With the coup, families who had cultivated the same plot of land for a hundred years and more were suddenly cast out of their homes, expelled from their land, and saw their belongings stripped from them, their men beaten, and their women assaulted. Overnight, Indians who had known no other land than Fiji, shopkeepers and farmers, found themselves living as refugees in their own country. In the following days, the mayhem spread. In the highlands of Viti Levu, Fijian landowners took over the Monasavu Dam, which supplied Suva and much of Fiji's population with electricity. Increase our payments, they said, or we'll blow it up. In Savusavu, on the island of Vanua Levu, the Air Fiji pilots were, inexplicably, taken hostage by Fijian nationalists. Turtle Island, a posh, American-owned resort in the Yasawa Islands, was seized by the indigenous landowners. The bewildered tourists were evacuated.

At the parliament, the long siege lasted fifty-six days. The president, Ratu Sir Kamisese Mara, who is revered in Fiji much as George Washington is in America, was compelled to resign. Elements of the Fijian military also mutinied. At the Queen Elizabeth barracks in Suva, members of the elite Counter-Revolutionary Warfare Unit turned on the soldiers who remained loyal to the government, killing four of them.

The repercussions of the coup were playing out as we arrived in Fiji. George Speight was eventually arrested and accused of treason. The Indian-led government he deposed, however, was not permitted to return to power. The chiefs in Fiji, who, despite an elected parliament, remained the true power in Fiji, appointed a caretaker government. Many of those presumed to have played a role in the coup found themselves posted to Fijian embassies abroad, as well as to the U.N. in New York.

Suva remained littered with the blackened shells of buildings torched during the looting that followed the coup. Police checkpoints had been set up on all the roads leading into town. And yet, as we began to settle in, a veneer of normalcy had returned to the city. The curfews had been lifted. Classes had resumed at the University of the South Pacific. Even the tourists were beginning to return to the sunny side of Fiji after the resorts slashed their prices.

As we ambled past the derelict hulk of the Pacific Grand Hotel, idly talking about what, precisely, I knew about the friendliness of the women of Suva, we noticed a Fijian man frantically beckoning us from across the road.

"I am Ahanda," he said once we had crossed the street. "This means Henry Cooper in English."

All right, we thought. Technically, my name could be translated as Johnny Comfort.

Ahanda was a security guard at the Pacific Grand Hotel. He had called out to us because he wanted to say hi. This was unusual in Fiji. Fijian men tend to be reserved, even rather regal in their bearing. They're not unfriendly, just inclined toward the formal. The colonial English and the Fijians had a great affinity for one another, or at least they did once the Fijians stopped eating Englishmen. Kings and queens, nobles and inherited privilege—these were concepts that meshed nicely with the Fijian chiefly system. Unlike the chiefs in much of Vanuatu, who are obliged to earn their position, Fijian chiefs are born to the manor.

There was, as far as we could tell, not much of the Pacific Grand left to guard. Built in 1914, the two-story hotel had once been the finest in Oceania, with stately colonnades and verandahs set to capture the breeze off Suva Harbor. Alas for the Pacific Grand, it was bought by Nauru, a grim flyspeck of a country that was once among the world's richest. After squandering the wealth it had derived from its phosphate deposits, Nauru was reduced to penury and today makes its living as a prison island housing Australia's illegal immigrants. The Pacific Grand Hotel, like most of the properties owned by Nauru throughout the Pacific, had been left to crumble.

"Would you like a tour?" Ahanda asked, prying apart the plywood shutters that had been nailed to the entranceway, presumably to keep people out. Ahanda, clearly, had a rather unique interpretation of his role as a security guard. Sylvia squeezed through, carefully maneuvering the volleyball she had evidently swallowed.

Inside, it was like stepping through a time warp and arriving the day after the Gilded Age had ended. The champagne flutes had been picked up, the chandeliers removed, but otherwise the lobby remained as it must have appeared to the fops and dandies of a bygone era. Well, provided, of course, that one ignored the pools of bird shit, the mounds of dust, the acres of cobwebs, and the uncomfortable feeling that, any moment now, you might fall through the floorboards.

"Come upstairs," Ahanda said. "I will show you something." We followed him up. *Creak, creak,* the stairs said ominously as we passed a sign informing us that the morning post left at 10 A.M. Pausing for a moment to pluck the cobwebs off our faces, we emerged onto the second-floor balcony. A dozen birds scattered into the air.

"You see?" Ahanda said. "This is where Queen Elizabeth stood. The first one. She stood like this." Ahanda struck a regal pose, surveying his domain with outstretched hands. "It's very beautiful."

It was.

Suva looked remarkably good when you directed your gaze away from it. The city was on a peninsula, unraveling in helter-skelter fashion over urban hills, tumbling toward the ocean that encased it on three sides. It became the capital of Fiji in 1882. A few Australian farmers had settled on the peninsula, and when their cotton crops failed, they were able to persuade the English government to move the capital from Levuka, on the island of Ovalau, to Suva, which offered more room for growth. "We have rain," the Australians told the English. "You'll love it." Today, some 350,000 people lived in the city, and from what I could tell, only four of them had garbage cans of their own. The remainder just dropped their trash on the sidewalks and waited for the wind to blow it to the town dump beside the WELCOME TO SUVA sign.

The hotel overlooked Suva Harbor, one of the most appealing deepwater anchorages in the Pacific. A thin white crescent of breakers marked where the reef lay. In the near distance were the remains of several boats that had misjudged the harbor entrance, their hulks slowly whittled away by the unrelenting waves. We could see the dim outlines of Beqa, a mountainous isle whose inhabitants have a peculiar fondness for walking on fire. Directly across was a wall of green mountains and the steep, jagged eminence called Joske's Thumb, named, naturally, after Mr. Joske's digit. On the lawn below us, we noticed a mongoose skirting the seawall. Mongooses were everywhere in Suva. They had been imported by the English, who had unleashed the rodentlike creatures to clear the sugarcane fields of rats. They also killed most of the snakes on Viti Levu, which I understand, in principle, was a really bad thing to do, particularly as the snakes were harmless, or so it is alleged.

"Come this way," Ahanda said. We followed him around the balcony until we reached the front of the hotel. From our perch, we found it remarkable how very English Suva appeared. Directly beside us was a lawn-bowling club. I had never before actually seen a lawn-bowling club and was pleased to find that the lawn bowlers met my expectations of what lawn bowlers ought to look like. Even in Fiji, the English dress code was enforced on the bowling green. Dressed in starched whites, the bowlers looked like male nurses assigned to a mental ward. Across the road stood the Fiji Museum and Thurston Gardens, a typically English park with a clock tower and a bandstand. It was overgrown with weeds, and as I had discovered during my week alone, it was the only place in the South Pacific that I knew of where one could reliably smell cannabis. Next to the gardens were manicured lawns that rose up a hillside toward Government House, the former residence of the colonial governor-general and, since independence, the home of the president of Fiji. The entrance was a tumble of barbed wire and tire spikes guarded by camouflaged Fijian soldiers carrying M-16s. Elsewhere we could see the old parliament building, a gray stone edifice that looked like a mausoleum and would not have been out of place in Manchester. Farther down Victoria Parade, where it became Queen Elizabeth Drive, were clapboard bungalows, like seaside English cottages, including one completely ensnared by vines, above which slept a thousand flying foxes, a stinking mass of bats dangling from tree limbs.

Directly across from the hotel, in the wide expanses of Albert Park, scores of Fijian men were busy pounding each other senseless.

"Do you play rugby?" Ahanda asked me.

I stared at the men. So this was rugby. I knew, of course, that rugby was not a game for sissies. In the U.S., however, one tends to think of it as a game played by men named Biff or Scooter, men deemed just a little too effete, a little too fey, for football. I had come to regard the game through the prism of class, envisioning players prancing about in bob haircuts and designer jerseys, lingering for perhaps a moment too long in the group embrace known as a scrum, hoping that, on the sidelines, Buffy wouldn't notice. Fijian rugby, however, was something different entirely. This was gleeful mayhem, with large, barefoot men colliding into each other like trucks at a demolition derby.

"No," I said. "I'm afraid I don't play rugby." I was a hockey man back in the day. "But it looks like the Fijians know how to play."

"Fiji is no good this year," Ahanda said. "The boys are lazy."

Ahanda was referring to the Fijian national team that played rugby sevens, an offshoot of the standard rugby game that features fifteen players per side. In rugby sevens, two teams of seven play each other for fourteen minutes rather than the standard eighty. It is typically played in tournament form, with teams playing through round-robins and on into quarter- and semifinals before the two top teams meet each other for a twenty-minute final. Each tournament lasts one day, so by the end, the two top teams have played roughly a half-dozen games. I, of course, didn't know anything at all about rugby, much less its more esoteric deviations. It wasn't until some days later that, through the open windows of our new house, we suddenly heard 350,000 people collectively gasp and hoot.

Our house, which we'd rented from an Indo-Fijian businessman, was on a hillside overlooking Laucala Bay. Below us, on the steep slopes, were Indo-Fijian land squatters living in tin shanties. Just above us lived a mixed-race family that owned Fiji's largest shipping company. Across the street was the enormous, rambling home of an Indo-Fijian man who owned one of the country's bus companies. Next to him lived a colonel in the Fijian army; his house was painted purple with black tiger stripes, like an animated dinosaur in camouflage. This was an astonishingly diverse neighborhood, but be they rich or poor, Indian or Fijian, something had gotten their attention. For a long minute there was silence, a highly unusual occurrence in Suva. And then we heard the groan of thousands, shortly to be followed by wild whooping.

"What do you think is going on?" Sylvia asked.

"I have absolutely no idea. Maybe Saki knows."

Saki was the night watchman. The landlord had insisted that he stay. We had agreed, since the last thing we wanted to do in post-coup Fiji was to take someone's job away, and also because Suva had become a dangerous town after dark. As usual, Saki was nattily attired. This was because it is my mother's mission to have me dressed like a country club golfer, and every year to that end I receive a package from her containing pleated trousers and collared polo shirts, which I dutifully pass on to anyone who will have them. Saki, I was fairly certain, was the only night watchman in Fiji wearing Ralph Lauren.

"Saki, what is everyone shouting about?" I asked.

"The rugby game," he said, resplendent in his yellow golf shirt. "It is the finals. Fiji against New Zealand."

He cocked his head, straining to hear the commentary from a thousand distant television sets. We too had a television, and in a moment of indulgence, we had signed up for the deluxe cable option, which allowed us to receive three channels: the Fijian national station, a channel that played old Bollywood movies around the clock, and a sports channel that seemed to specialize in Korean ping-pong and Malaysian high school basketball. I turned on the game.

"Do you want to come in and watch?" I asked Saki.

"No, no. I'll stay outside."

I turned the TV so that he could watch the action from the open doorway. To my great surprise, I found the game riveting. Several of the Fijian players had tourniquets around their head. They were stained crimson. I didn't think I had ever seen such a fluid game before, with the action moving seamlessly from defense to offense. This was the finals of the Hong Kong Sevens, one of a dozen stops the annual tournament played throughout the year. Even Sylvia, in a first for her, found herself rooting for a sports team on television. "This is so much better than football," she said. I wasn't ready to go that far. I had invested many a Sunday afternoon in watching football, and I wasn't prepared to admit that perhaps there had been better things I could have done with my time.

"He's a farmer from Tailevu," Saki noted after a Fijian player scored a try. There were other farmers on the team, as well as prison guards. A small island nation fielding a team of farmers and prison guards is a hard one to root against, especially when the New

Zealand All Blacks were professionals. Fiji, alas, to the collective groan of a nation, lost the game.

"The boys are no good this year," Saki said, shaking his head.

What did he mean? I wondered. Even I knew that the New Zealand All Blacks were perennial world champions in rugby. Simply reaching the tournament finals, I thought, was a mighty fine showing for Fiji.

"Last year, Fiji was the world champion," Saki noted sadly.

"Really."

This would become the common refrain over the rugby season, a national sigh of disappointment as Fiji proved unable to overtake New Zealand and South Africa in the world rankings. But that was the remarkable thing about Fijian rugby. Though the game was played solely by Fijians, who by and large tend to make all other nationalities appear scrawny and meek, the country as a whole— Indo-Fijians, Chinese, Europeans—rooted for its team as one. Now, call me sentimental, but given that the country had recently been torn asunder by a coup led by Fijian nationalists toppling an Indian-led government, I thought this was a rather hopeful sign. Peace and understanding through violent sport.

Determined to do our share in promoting harmony among the peoples of the world, we invited a number of new friends—Fijians, Indo-Fijians, other Pacific Islanders, Australians, and Brits—to our house to watch the American Super Bowl, which was being broadcast on the cable sports station just after a junior badminton tournament in Jakarta. Sylvia couldn't give a hoot about American football—never has and, I can safely say, never will. Still, I thought it might be fun. I'm not sure why. I couldn't recall a single Super Bowl party I had attended as being any fun before the fourth beer.

There was another reason I was eager to watch the Super Bowl, however. One predawn September morning in Vanuatu, we had received a phone call from Chuck, an American colleague of Sylvia's who also lived in Vila. "Turn on your TV," he said. "The World Trade Center's been destroyed. The Pentagon's been hit. America's been attacked. It's worse than Pearl Harbor." Only the day before, Chuck had informed us that in his youth he had made his living as an acid dealer. I looked at the clock. It wasn't even 4 A.M. Acid flashback, I thought irritably.

"Who was it," Sylvia groaned.

"It was Chuck, reminding us to just say no to drugs."

"Huh?"

"He said something about America being attacked, the World Trade Center, the Pentagon. Crazy talk."

And then we turned on the television.

Though we were on a distant island, far away from the madness and tragedy, we felt connected to the events unfolding on the other side of the planet. Partly, this was because we were from Washington, D.C. In the weeks that followed, I'd find myself taking the packages of baby clothes sent to us by friends and family in Washington and opening them outside, paying careful attention to wind direction, lest I release a billowing cloud of anthrax. But the connection, of course, was deeper. While I wasn't an American citizen—the paperwork is such a hassle—I was culturally an American. As most Americans who have lived abroad can appreciate, defending American culture can be a tedious experience. Americans, we are told, are fat, vapid, culturally illiterate, money-obsesssed, hegemonic demons. And so much more, I say. Now, with the entire world expressing their solidarity with America, here, I thought was a perfect opportunity to share a little American culture: the Super Bowl.

The game, the announcers declared, was being viewed by a billion people around the world. I couldn't really say whether that was true, but I was fairly confident that all fifteen people watching in Fiji were gathered in our living room. If there were a billion people watching, quite likely many of them were as agape as we were watching the pregame show. It's funny how deranged America can appear when you've been out of the country for a while. Here were fighter jets screaming across the sky, merging seamlessly into the Budweiser logo. American soldiers, taking a moment from the toil of fighting a war in Afghanistan, introduced the football players as the announcers anticipated the tough battle ahead on the gridiron. The Stars and Stripes billowed in the breeze. A commercial suggested that now might be a good time to buy an SUV. Seventy thousand fans sang a stirring rendition of the national anthem. Tears welled. The cameras turned to the soldiers watching from an overseas base. A sponsor reminded us to drink lite beer. The announcers spoke of patriotism and sacrifice as dozens of enormous multimillionaires wobbled onto the field to play a game. Military helicopters buzzed overhead. A coin was tossed. The Super Bowl started. And collectively a billion people fell asleep.

American football, I was startled to discover, is a mind-numbingly boring game to watch. I spent a few minutes trying to explain the rules. "Why do they wear helmets?" asked Savuto, a Fijian woman who worked with Sylvia. "So that they don't get hurt," I replied. I could see Savuto thinking: *Sissy-boys.*

"Why are they just standing around?"

"That's called a huddle," I said. "This is where they talk about what to do next."

"But they keep doing the same thing. All the fat ones fall down, and then the little one with the ball runs into them and falls down too."

She had a point. Perhaps I had become corrupted by the ceaseless action of rugby sevens, but football now struck me as an artless spectacle performed by obese men in tights. After the babes, bombs, and beer razzle-dazzle of the pregame show, the actual game seemed like a colossal anticlimax. Perhaps the Super Bowl wasn't an ideal forum for promoting peace and understanding among the peoples of the world.

"Do you have a sock?" James asked. James was a Ni-Vanuatu carpenter I had befriended over a kava bowl at the home of a mutual acquaintance.

"A sock?"

"For the kava."

"Ah . . . of course."

I had remained loyal to the kava from Vanuatu, and it wasn't long after we arrived in Fiji that I found the stall in the covered market that sold it. James respected my sophisticated palate, and now and then we had a sock or two of kava together. Soon we were all gathered around the kava bowl, men and women of disparate cultures sitting on woven mats on a balcony overlooking the island where George Speight was imprisoned, and as the sky reddened with the sun's descent, I knew that at least here, on a hillside in Suva, peace and harmony reigned.

CHAPTER 11

In which the author discovers, shortly after rising from his slumbers, that his backyard has disappeared and that it can be found residing by the shanty down the hill, leaving in its place a cavernous chasm upon which his house is delicately perched, a circumstance that provides him with one more reason to take a holiday, to get away from it all, and so with his wife he travels far, far away to Fiji—that is, the Other Fiji.

ONE OF THE GREAT ADVANTAGES OF LIVING IN FIJI, OF course, was living in Fiji. Suva, with its pervasive sense of doom and gloom, was technically in Fiji, but now and then, whenever events warranted, we had a hankering for the Other Fiji, the one George Clooney visited. Though still a rare sight in Suva, tourists had begun to return to the islands. For the visitors lounging around the resort pools, the coup was something the hotel employees whispered about as they fetched another round of daiquiris. As they admired the ocean vista from a verandah, local politics, no doubt, was the furthest thing from their minds. This was paradise, after all. And I understood. We too enjoyed the vista, even in Suva. From our house, we had a view of Nukulau Island, a picturesque islet that had once been the Suva equivalent of Central Park in New York, an outlet for urban steam. It was a picnic island, a place where the inhabitants of Suva took their families for an afternoon of swimming and frolicking. Regrettably, the island had now been transformed into a prison for George Speight and his fellow conspirators.

Though we couldn't escape this reminder of recent events, we appreciated the view nevertheless. Most mornings, I settled myself on the balcony with my laptop, and as my eyes passed over the slums below and the navy patrol boat ferrying supplies to the prisoners, I'd recall our lives in Kiribati. I had found a publisher for my book, which was very exciting. "See," I had told Sylvia, "I *can* earn a living." More important, I now had an answer for my offspring. We had intuited correctly: a sonogram had revealed that Sylvia was carrying a boy. Years from now, I envisioned him asking, "I know Mom was working when I was born, but what did you do?" I had been worried that I'd have nothing more to say than a mumbled "writing" as I set off for my job manning the deep fryer. I might still be destined for the deep fryer, I thought, but at least I'd have a book to show the little one, though it occurred to me, as I finished a chapter on the mating habits of dogs in Kiribati, that I might not let him read it until he turned eighteen.

One morning, as we brought our coffee to the balcony we sensed that something was amiss. The view had been strangely altered. We felt somehow *higher*. It had rained throughout the night, but now the sun shone brightly. There was clarity, too much clarity. Everything seemed so much more open. *Hey,* I thought, *there used to be a tree there.* Peering over the edge of the balcony, we gasped and instinctively retreated back into the house. While we had slept, our backyard had disappeared. All of it. Where once there had been a gentle hillside planted with banana trees, coconut trees, and cassava, now there was air.

"Are we safe here?" Sylvia asked.

I had no idea. We had heard nothing, felt nothing. I cautiously returned to the balcony. While just the day before it had been a mere ten-foot drop to the ground below, we were now perched above a fifty-foot chasm. Looking down, I was suddenly horrified to see where the tons of mud and debris had fallen. Below us lived a family of Indo-Fijian land squatters. Their house was a tin-and-plywood shanty without plumbing or electricity. The mud slide had buried it up to its windows.

"Is everyone all right?" I yelled. Two men were busy with shovels, digging the house out from under the debris.

"Everyone okay," one of them called back.

I seized a shovel and scrambled down the hillside, following the edge of the colossal pit the landslide had created. Looking up, our house seemed to be teetering on the edge of the abyss. The mud slide had sheared off the hill to within a few feet of the house's foundations.

"You must build a retaining wall," said Vijay, a laborer who lived in the mud-encrusted house. A few weeks earlier, five people had died in a mud slide on Rabi, the small Fijian island that the British had given to the I-Kiribati expelled from Banaba Island, which had long ago been rendered uninhabitable by phosphate mining. As we had learned in Vanuatu, mud slides were an ever-present threat on the hilly islands of the South Pacific.

I began helping the family clear the debris, feeling awful about the situation. Here we were, guests in their country, and look at the mess we had made. Thank goodness, I reflected, that no one had been injured. Fortunately, our landlord agreed to build a retaining wall. Unfortunately, the retaining wall was built on island time, and during the subsequent weeks and months, as the workers followed a schedule known only to themselves, we'd find ourselves huddling in the back of the house whenever it rained, fearful that our weight alone would prove to be the tipping point that sent the house hurtling down the hill. Here, we thought, was one more very good reason to get out of Suva, and whenever we could, we hopped into our clunky secondhand car and set a course for the sun.

It was a bewilderingly odd juxtaposition of worlds. One moment we were at home, fearful of the house toppling off the hill, half-expecting to hear an exchange of gunfire as the trial of George Speight got under way, and the next moment we'd find ourselves on the west side of Viti Levu, that other world of beaches and deluxe resorts, contemplating which of the glimmering offshore islands we fancied going to for a swim. These were the Mamanucas, a group of small coral islands fringed with white-sand beaches. They look exactly as one expects islands in the South Pacific to look, possibly because the Mamanucas and, a little farther out, the Yasawas, are the preferred locations for films set on tropical islands—movies like *Castaway* and *Blue Lagoon*. Once the tourists began to return to Fiji, the Mamanucas were back in business.

The names of the individual islands alone suggested that this, very possibly, was not exactly the real Fiji. There's Castaway Island, Beachcomber Island, Bounty Island, South Sea Island, and Treasure Island, among others. That's all right, we thought. We lived in the real Fiji, and now and then, we wanted off. We decided one day to go to Beachcomber Island, which we soon discovered was an excellent place to go to if you're in your thirties and, just for the fun of it, you want to spend a few hours feeling really old. From our hotel on the main island, we hopped onto a sputtering bus and proceeded to spend the next hour and a half stopping at a dozen hotels to pick up every shirtless backpacker in the greater Nadi area. Beachcomber Island, apparently, was a mecca for backpackers living out a fantasy of young adulthood, a fantasy I had deeply envied when I was fifteen.

As we approached the island by high-speed catamaran, the smell of diesel gave way to the odor of sunscreen radiating off a hundred bodies draped in the sun. From a distance, the island looked like a wildlife sanctuary for pink seals. What else would be flopping about under the midday sun? Like most Pacific Islanders, we had come to regard sunbathing as one of those peculiar things that foreigners do. As we stepped ashore it became clear that many of the figures lying prone on the beach were sleeping off the excesses of the previous night. Beachcomber Island was, as the kids like to say, a place to party. At least a third of the slumbering bodies had horrific sunburns. Many of the women were topless, though there was a large sign stating that topless sunbathing was really un-Fijian, so please keep your bikinis on, we're Methodists. "That's going to hurt," Sylvia said, nodding toward one woman whose breasts were toasted medium rare.

Apparently, while we had been living abroad, someone had sent a missive to all Western women under the age of twenty-five: *Put a large tattoo above your butt.* Another directive must have been sent to the men: *Tattoo barbed wire around your arm.* As far as I could tell, resistance had been futile. We went for a swim and enjoyed the looks that the island's other guests gave Sylvia, who was in a bikini. You couldn't tell she was pregnant from behind, but then she'd swing her ballooning belly around and we'd hear the gasps. We could see them thinking, *I hope that's not contagious.*

Beachcomber Island was a speck of an island, easily circumnavigated in five minutes. It had a beach, a few palm trees, a large dormitory filled with bunk beds, and a bar. "Bunk 83, please come to the bar," someone said over the loudspeakers. Bunk 83? It sounded like hell to me.

Very clearly, we had passed through some invisible barrier, some passage that prevented us from seeing the appeal of sharing a large dorm room with a hundred people in various states of inebriation. We felt deeply out of our element, possibly even more so than the Japanese couple wearing inscrutable T-shirts. IRONY, declared the woman's baseball cap. WORK HARDER, said her T-shirt. Okay, I thought, I get it. I think. But what about her friend? He wore a T-shirt with an image of a bottle of soy sauce. SOY SAUCE, it said. What did that mean?

Waiting for the boat to take us back to the main island, we settled at a table near the bar and eavesdropped on a couple of flirtatious youngsters. "I really like beef," said the boy.

"Do you eat wheat bread?" asked the girl.

"Not really," he said.

"How about vegetables? What's your favorite?"

"Um . . . I guess potato. I like french fries a lot. But what I really like is beef."

This went on for a half hour. It was strangely riveting, even endearing, and as we left we hoped that they'd find happiness and perhaps attend Homecoming together.

We too wanted to feel young, and so on our next trip to the sunny side of Fiji, we booked a passage through the Yasawa Islands on the Blue Lagoon Cruise. It was very pleasant, and as we hopped from island to island we felt our youth restored.

"So you don't own a house?" asked Bill as dolphins skipped above the waves. Bill and his wife, Susan, were from California.

"No. We just rent."

"It's probably too late for you, then."

"Too late?"

"Let's see," Bill said. "We bought our house back in ninety-eight for $525,000. Today it's worth $1.3 million."

"More like $1.5 million," Susan added. "Remember, Sven and Jean sold theirs for $1.3 million, and we have more square footage."

"How many square feet do you have?" asked Jim. He and his wife, Katherine, were from Massachusetts.

Bill told him. "So that works out to about $415 a square foot.

We're roughly at $375 where we live. I bought a house last month that I plan on flipping when it gets to $400."

"Wow," Katherine said to us. "So you're going to have a baby and you don't even own your home?"

It was just what we needed. Suddenly we felt like a couple of reckless kids, footloose and fancy-free.

Eventually, we found a place where we felt neither too young nor too old. Among Sylvia's programs was a coral-restoration project near Sigatoka on Viti Levu's Coral Coast. Because of changes in the water temperature, the coral in front of the Fijian Resort was bleached, and Sylvia's organization was involved in attempts to restore its health. Whenever she traveled to the project site, she stayed at the resort. I accompanied her because . . . well, because I could. The Fijian was a family resort, and when Sylvia was free, we studied the families. After all, we were soon to become one ourselves. "What you really need to be doing," a kindly Australian woman told Sylvia, "is sleeping." This struck Sylvia as an excellent plan, preferable to the one I had concocted for the afternoon. I had hoped to visit the Sigatoka Sand Dunes, an archeological site where the shifting sands were continuously unearthing bones and pottery that dated from Fiji's earliest settlers some three thousand years ago.

"I don't think so," Sylvia told me. "It's, what, ninety-five degrees today?"

"It's a little toasty," I agreed.

"And I'm eight months pregnant."

"Indeed you are."

"Well, I could waddle up and down sand dunes in the blistering sun. Or I could turn the air conditioning on and have a nap. Not much of a choice for me. So I'll see you later. Have fun."

I drove our little Toyota a few miles down toward the dunes, nearly colliding with an errant cow. It made driving the Queen's Road particularly exciting, knowing that around every curve there might lurk an eight-hundred-pound ruminant. I parked the car in the shade near the ranger's station and began marching up the wooded incline. The air reeked of burning rubbish from the nearby town dump. What was it about dumps in Fiji? I wondered. Why would anyone place a burning town dump beside one of the most important archeological sites in the Pacific? As I crested the hillside and emerged from the woods my nostrils burned and my eyes watered from the smoke. Really, I thought, they should just appoint me emperor of Fiji and we'd have a swift end to such things. Despite the burning air, I paused to read the information plaques in front of various trees. One in particular I found notable. It was for a small tree called a *vau,* which among its uses included: "An infusion of the leaves is also given as a tonic to mothers after childbirth to prevent a relapse."

A relapse? Like a relapse of shingles? Then it occurred to me that this was a very sensitive way of saying that the ancient Fijians used contraceptives.

I moseyed on and finally encountered the dunes. Rising more than a hundred feet, sand dunes of these dimensions are not typical of the South Pacific. In this case, however, the Sigatoka River lay a few miles distant, and over an eon or two, it had carried sediment toward the ocean. The freshwater prevented coral from forming, and the waves pushed the sediment back toward the beach, where the wind had carved it into the massive dunes found today.

I stepped onto the sand, and soon I was madly hopping about—*hot, hot, hot.* Though I was wearing sandals, the sand was scalding. Clearly, marching up sand dunes on a hot, sunny afternoon in Fiji was not the wisest thing to do. *Hurts, hurts, hurts.* I sprinted up the face of the dune. It was agonizing. At the top, where wind swept in over the ocean, the sand was tolerable to stand on, and I spent a moment fanning my feet. Looking down, I saw something. Could it be? It was about a foot long, alabaster white, broad and tapered at the ends. As I stumbled down the dune I noticed that the object was sharp with serrated edges. Was this an artifact? Had I stumbled across some ancient relic? I picked it up. Should I just leave it there, I wondered, and inform an expert of my find? They'd probably want to arrange a dig in this spot. But if I just left it there, the wind would soon cover it with sand, and this, this . . . find might be lost forever.

After much deliberation, I carried it back with me toward the beach. Who had been the last person to use this implement? I wondered. A chief? A cannibal? Was this perhaps used to carve human flesh? I followed the path along the beach. A stiff breeze whipped up whitecaps on the ocean. An arrow pointed me toward a trail leading back to the road. I noticed a man studiously reading a plaque in front of what appeared to be a very unremarkable tree.

"Look what I found," I said with giddy enthusiasm. "What do you think it might be?"

He took it in his hands and pondered it for a moment. "It's a cuttlefish," he said in a thick Scottish brogue.

Great, I thought. Just when I needed one, I had run into a Scottish naturalist.

"Ah," I said. "I know that many Pacific Islanders used fish bones as tools."

He gazed attentively, no doubt amazed by my knowledge.

"The I-Kiribati, for instance," I went on, "used fish bones for hooks and shark teeth for swords. They even put blowfish on their heads, using them like helmets."

"Well," he said, studying the relic. "It is calcified. You should take your find to the park ranger."

My thoughts exactly. I trudged on through a more wooded area. There was a cacophony of noise, like a thousand rattling rattlesnakes. Were the gods displeased?

When I arrived at the ranger station, I showed the relic to the Fijian woman there. She seemed amused.

"Is the ranger in?" I asked.

"No," she said. "He's in Suva."

Excellent, I thought. I was headed back to Suva the following day. "Do you think I might be able to bring this to him in Suva?"

"You want to bring this to the park ranger in Suva?"

"Yes, if it's not too much trouble. I understand, though, if you want to keep it here."

"No," she said with a laugh. "You may take it to Suva."

She wrote down the appropriate address. It seemed a trifle irresponsible to let a stranger wander off with what might very well be an important discovery illuminating the history of the ancient Fijians. Nevertheless, I happily drove off with my artifact.

I found Sylvia sitting by the pool at the Fijian, chatting amicably with the Australian woman who had recommended rigorous napping for the last weeks of pregnancy. "This is Beth," Sylvia said, introducing us.

"Look what I found," I said, showing them my discovery. "I'm taking it to the park ranger in Suva."

"You're bringing a cuttlefish bone to the park ranger?" Beth asked, looking at me rather oddly. How is it, I wondered, that everyone around here seems to know what a cuttlefish is?

"Well," I said, "I think it might be very old. And did you look at the sharp edges? It looks like a tool to me."

"We give them to budgies to gnaw on."

"Budgies?"

"It's a pet bird. They love chewing on cuttlebones."

"But . . . how would this cuttlebone find its way over a hundred-foot sand dune?" I asked.

"They're very light," Beth said. "The wind probably blew it. Why don't you smell it?"

To my dismay, it smelled like dead fish.

CHAPTER 12

In which a child is born, causing much bewilderment for his parents, though fortunately they are soon set straight by Anna, who shows them how to raise a child island-style.

ONE MORNING, WHILE I WAS BROWSING THROUGH THE bookstore at the University of the South Pacific in Suva, I came across a book called *Misconceptions,* by the writer Naomi Wolf. There had once been a bookstore in Nuku'alofa, the capital of Tonga, but it had burned down, leaving the USP bookstore as the last remaining outpost of literature in the South Pacific. Very often, a shop in Fiji would decide to call itself a bookstore, but invariably it sold little more than stationery. As the sole proprietor of books in Oceania, the USP bookshop had a remarkably small selection, a fact that caused me no great loss of sleep. I do not respond well to too much choice, and very often in the U.S., whenever I set foot inside a book emporium containing thousands of titles, I'd leave empty-handed, confounded by options. Choice was not a problem in Suva, however, and presented with so little to choose from, I bought whatever caught my eye. *Misconceptions* was about the author's experiences with motherhood. Well, isn't that something, I thought. Sylvia was on the cusp of motherhood, and so I purchased the book, thinking that she might like to read a little about what awaited her.

At home, I dipped into the book, idly scanning its pages. And then I began to read it more thoroughly. Apparently, motherhood wasn't so wonderful. Indeed, motherhood sounded grim and awful, a curse borne by women.

"Where's that book you got?" Sylvia asked.

"Uh . . . I don't know," I lied.

In truth, I had hidden the book in the deepest recesses of a closet. This was no time for negativity. I had no idea what having a baby entailed. Indeed, the very idea of having a child still seemed a little amorphous to me. I did, of course, realize that something was afoot. Despite evidence to the contrary, I knew that Sylvia hadn't swallowed a basketball. But still, the knowledge that there was a baby on the way seemed nebulous at best. All I knew was that it was important to be chipper.

Sylvia had had a happy pregnancy, and she was at her happiest when I'd arrive home with takeout from the Hare Krishna Restaurant. It had become extreme, this fixation with food from the Hare Krishnas, and I feared that our son might be destined for the airports. Now and then, of course, we'd come across someone determined to dent our optimism. "I can't believe you're having your child in Fiji," wagged an American nurse at the Fourth of July party at the U.S. Embassy. Well, Naomi Wolf didn't make having a baby in the U.S. sound so peachy either, I thought. In the U.S., as I understood, a pregnant woman was subject to a barrage of tests, many with a high likelihood of false positives or ambiguous results. I couldn't imagine what it would be like to know that your child had a 19 percent chance of developing Down syndrome, a 22 percent chance of spina bifida, and a high likelihood of developing male-pattern baldness and a hairy back. What is it that doctors expect women to do with such information, except go into angst overload? Fortunately for us, this wasn't a problem in Fiji, because there was no high-tech testing done in Fiji.

As the due date neared, Sylvia's checkups were upped to once a week. Her doctor was the indefatigable Dr. Brown, a Fijian doctor from the Lau Islands, one of the handful of doctors who had remained in Fiji after the coup, when many of the Indian doctors took their cue and emigrated. Her office was spare and perpetually teeming with patients. The doctors may have left, but the babies kept coming. It was like being in a Benetton ad. The women were Fijian, Asian, and Indian. One woman was even shrouded in a black burka.

We had long ago learned to ignore the can of roach spray Dr. Brown kept in her office. This was the tropics, after all. At the final checkup, Dr. Brown informed us that the baby was breech.

"Maybe he will turn," she said. "They sometimes do. But if he doesn't, I think we should do a C-section. If you were a large Fijian woman with wide hips, I would say maybe we could try to do it naturally, but you are a skinny *kaivalangi,* and breech births can be very dangerous."

She flashed us a significant look. She knew about kaivalangis and their books, all of which seemed to state that a natural, drug-free delivery was a beautiful experience and that a woman will never truly be a woman until she pushes through a baby unaided by painkillers and preferably, doctors, accompanied only by fragrant candles, new age music, a bathtub, and someone who calls herself a doula.

"Don't be a hero, darling," I said.

Sylvia laughed. The only aspect of delivering a child that had appealed to her was the prospect of taking a heavy hit of morphine. She more or less sighed in relief at the idea of a C-section.

We took note of the baby's position, calculated when he would be fully cooked, and scheduled the operation for a Monday at 1 P.M., a very civilized hour for having a baby. I was hoping to avoid a midnight dash to the hospital.

As we found ourselves far away from the wisdom of grand-mothers, we thought it prudent to ask for help, for the baby's sake as much as ours. Anna was a kindly woman who lived in the village of Wailoko, outside Suva. Like Anna, most of the residents of Wailoko were descendants of Solomon Islanders who had been brought to Fiji by the British to help build the roads. No wonder the Fijians looked so fondly upon the British. They brought in Indians to cul-tivate the land and Solomon Islanders to build the infrastructure, while the Fijians themselves were encouraged to do nothing more than collect the rents. Anna had four grown children of her own, and for many years she had worked as a nanny for expatriate fami-lies. She *knew* babies.

"*Uuuueee,* Sylvia," she said one afternoon, with her customary glimmer. "You are having a baby tonight."

What's this?

"Anna," I said. "If this baby has my genes, then there's no way he's going to be early for anything." I myself had been born two weeks late, a fact that surprises no one who knows me.

"You are a silly man," Anna scoffed.

And lo, at midnight, I awoke to the words I dreaded hearing.

"My water broke," Sylvia said.

Men, I discovered, are hardwired for this moment. There is no lingering here. The sleep just dissipates. Every pore of my being was devoted to getting Sylvia out of the house pronto and into the arms of trained professionals. I was on the phone a millisecond later.

"Dr. Brown? . . . Is that you? . . . You have to wake up . . . Hello? . . . Dr. Brown? Sylvia's water broke. The baby's coming."

"Well, you better bring her in, then," said Dr. Brown groggily.

Moments later we screeched to a halt in front of the hospital, a brand-new private hospital. "First World Care in a Third World Set-ting," said the brochure. Or something like that. Planned before the coup, the modest hospital—elsewhere it would be called a clinic—had been designed to lure the patients in the South Pacific who might otherwise choose to seek medical care in Australia or New Zealand.

"Hello? Anybody there?"

I shook the security guard awake from his kava dream.

"My wife's having a baby!" Sylvia stood calmly holding her belly. "Is Dr. Brown here? Is there a nurse? . . . Do you speak English?"

He did not.

"Baby," I said, pointing to Sylvia. "You know? . . . *Waaa, waaa.*"

The security guard shuffled off to get a nurse. Meanwhile, Sylvia was overtaken by a contraction. Her fingers dug deep into my arm. *Oh, god,* I thought. "Uh . . . okay," I panted. "Um . . . deep breath . . . uh . . . now exhale."

Finally, the nurse arrived, and soon we found ourselves in the birthing room, awaiting the arrival of the doctor.

At 4 a.m.—4 a.m. again!—Lukas emerged into this world, bawling and screaming.

"He looks like you," said the nurse. Frankly, like all newborns, he looked like the creature from the Black Lagoon. But what a wonder he was.

THERE IS BEFORE AND AFTER. And the change is startling. One day, you go to sleep with the reliable expectation that when you next arise, a new day will have begun. And then—after—you go to sleep, having first spent a long while cooing over the little angel slumbering in the crib next to you, and suddenly, from the depths of your dreams, you find yourself hurtling toward the ceiling, shaken to the core by the ferocious wail of a hungry infant.

"Wha . . . who . . . what's going on?" I sputtered, once I'd pried myself off the ceiling fan. After Lukas was born, Sylvia had remained in the hospital for four nights, attended by a platoon of nurses. Our boy was one of the first babies to be born in the new hospital, and Sylvia and Lukas were treated like celebrities. I had spent those first days in the hospital and my nights at home. Now, finally, the whole family was together.

"He's hungry," Sylvia said as she rose to get the howling baby.

"Well . . . what should we do?"

"Feed him, of course."

"Okay," I said. The baby continued to wail, a cry that pierced my soul. I wanted, more than anything, for the baby to be happy, to know that we were there for him, and to realize that while he might be out of the womb, he remained in a cocoon of love. Also, I really wanted him to stop crying. Even my bones rattled.

"What can I do? . . . Maybe you should hold him like . . . Or try . . ."

Breastfeeding was still a new experience for both mother and child, and while Sylvia remained serene, Lukas grew impatient. I sensed that he wanted his umbilical cord back.

"You know what you should do?" Sylvia said as I fluttered anxiously around her.

"Tell me. What can I do?"

"You should have a Nicorette."

Unsurprisingly, the cold-turkey method had not worked for me at all. *The baby's not here yet,* I had reasoned in the months since we'd arrived in Fiji, which meant that I could still . . . smoke. Yippee! But he was here now, and I quickly stuffed a wad of Nicorette in my mouth, seeking to get a grip on my frayed nerves.

Eventually, of course, like all parents, I grew accustomed to the midnight wail. After Sylvia fed him, Lukas would be handed over to me so that he'd have a warm shoulder to spit up on. Whereas once I had been repelled by the smell of vomit, now I took it as my natural odor. In the predawn darkness, I'd take him outside into the warm stillness of the Fijian night, and having discovered that my repertoire of lullabies consisted of little more than a line or two of dimly remembered Dutch children's songs, I'd sing him a medley of U2 songs from the eighties as Saki, the night watchman, gazed at us approvingly.

Lukas grew to be very comfortable on my shoulder. Indeed, he was at ease on anyone's shoulder. He took it as his natural state. This is because in Fiji, a child's feet never touch the ground. Babies are adored on the islands. We'd enter a restaurant, and the moment we arrived, a waitress would divest us of our son. "Where's the baby?" my mother asked in a panic when she visited a couple of months later.

"I don't know," I said.

"I think the bartender took him," Sylvia said.

My mother looked at us oddly. "You're going to have a hard time when you return to the U.S. As a general rule, in the U.S. we don't let strangers walk off with babies."

"But we're in Fiji," I said.

"I know," my mother said. "Couldn't you at least wear something nice, though? What happened to the clothes I sent you?"

It was astonishing how warm Fijians were with children. No matter if we were in a village or at a resort, soon Lukas would find himself shepherded from shoulder to shoulder. Sweet songs would be sung in his ear. Rugby players would coo and play peekaboo. In response, he'd gurgle appreciatively.

At home, Anna taught us everything we needed to know. Bewildered at first by our son's mysterious ways, we had simply listened attentively as she explained the nuances of burping and what, precisely, constituted a good poop. Whenever we had a question, she was there for us.

"I can't figure out why he's crying," I said one day. I had ruled out food, a heavy diaper, and sleep.

"It is because someone is thinking bad thoughts about him," Anna informed us. The three of us exchanged looks. "Not in here. Someone out there," she said, gesturing beyond the house.

The bastard, I thought. Now why would someone do that?

The months passed, and they were happy months. Here and there, we had our worries. Lukas's doctor was a Hare Krishna, and during the exams, the baby would take an inordinate interest in the poster of Lord Krishna. This will require close watching, I thought.

"You should massage the skull," the doctor told us, "to make it nice and round."

This we declined to do. Indians, apparently, prized round skulls, just as the Malekulans once favored elongated heads. As far as we could tell, Lukas's head was perfect as it was. And if he grew up to have a Winnebago head like his father, I was sure he'd get used to it.

By the time Lukas had passed his sixth month, we had come to conclude that Anna had the strength of Atlas. It is one thing to spend your day traipsing about with a seven-pound baby. It is altogether different when he is twenty pounds. Indeed, I myself grew weary after an hour. Sensing that he was sound asleep on my aching shoulder, I'd gently lay him in his crib, and the moment he touched the sheet, he'd let me know in that voluble way babies have that he didn't think this was a good idea. In a Fijian household, of course, there would be an endless supply of well-rested arms to take turns carrying a slumbering child. But we didn't quite live in a Fijian household. Thoughtlessly, we had failed to bring a village of cousins and aunties of our own to the South Pacific.

Lukas soon adjusted to the two worlds he inhabited. Eventually, we had our way of doing things while Anna had hers. We'd try to teach him Western ways, to become independent, while Anna coddled him island-style. "Babies shouldn't cry," she said, swooping him into her arms. Meanwhile, stopwatch in hand, Sylvia and I would stand just outside his door and spend long, wrenching minutes listening to him cry until, finally, he learned that not only could he nap in his crib; he could even sleep soundly through the night. Anna, however, insisted that he snooze on her shoulder. When we fed him pureed mango, he sat in a high chair. When Anna fed him, he sat in her lap. Anna sang Fijian lullabies. Concerned about what "Sunday, Bloody Sunday" might do to his psyche, I moved on to the ABC song.

We had come to believe that nothing was more revered in Fiji than a baby. I had begun to refer to him as our little *ratu,* or chief, and when, one evening, we were invited to attend a party at the neighbor's house, I looked forward to introducing our ratu to the other ratus who gathered there each evening to drink kava. In Fiji, kava is pounded, rather than ground, as it is in Vanuatu, and in the afternoons, throughout Suva, the air carried the *clang-clang* of kava being prepared. That night, while the kava was being pounded, a fleet of high-end SUVs arrived at the neighbor's house to deposit some of Fiji's highest-ranking chiefs. Our neighbor was a commoner, but as the owner of the country's largest shipping company, he was wealthy and clearly well connected.

With Lukas in my arms, I ambled next door.

"Come," said our jovial neighbor. "The ladies are inside. And the boys are over there, watching the game." He gestured to what appeared to be a shed. "I'll introduce you to the boys, and you can have a few shells."

Social occasions in Fiji, we found, often had a time-warp feel to them. The 1960s had never happened here; the men would gather around the kava bowl, and women were expected to cluster among themselves and talk about whatever it is that women talk about—casserole recipes, presumably.

"Do you want me to take the baby?" Sylvia asked.

"No, it's all right. I'll take him to meet the boys."

Inside the shed, the chiefs were gathered around a television. A rugby game was on. New Zealand versus Australia.

"A shell?" offered a rotund man in a formal sulu.

"Thank you," I said, taking the proffered kava. Lukas immediately reached for it. "Not until you're at least two years old."

"This is Ratu V," said my neighbor. "And that is Ratu I, and Ratu S, and Ratu T, and, of course, Ratu L."

A lot of ratus. I recognized a few of them. They were ministers in the caretaker government. I had, apparently, stumbled across the proverbial backroom. There was a lot of power in this room. If I were a Fijian commoner, I would have been trembling. One wrong word, an inopportune gesture, and I could shame my family's name forever. But I wasn't a Fijian commoner. I was just a regular commoner.

"Nice to meet you. And this is Lukas," I said, raising the baby. He warbled and drooled his acknowledgments. "He's my ratu."

Silence. Cold, hard glares. The chiefs regarded me with undisguised hostility. Lukas drooled some more.

I had apparently made a faux pas. I hadn't meant to cause offense. Come on, guys, I thought, it was just a little joke. Lighten up. But they didn't lighten up. No doubt, if this had happened in the past, they'd be sharpening their cannibal forks. Instead, they turned their attention back to the game. The ratus had homes in Australia and New Zealand, and they followed the game with interest. The kava was generously dished out. But not to me.

Well, I thought as I slipped back outside with Lukas. It was true what I said. "You are my chief," I said to him.

He grunted magnanimously.

When I told Anna about the encounter, she laughed mirthfully.

"Ratu Lukas," she chuckled, taking the baby. "I do not think you will be drinking kava with the ratus again."

CHAPTER 13

In which the author travels to Savusavu on the island of Vanua Levu, a journey that causes him to reconsider his aversion to flying, and while exploring the island he discovers that even here, in what might be called paradise, there are many yearning for escape.

O NE MORNING, I FOUND MYSELF IN THE OFFICES OF Consort Shipping. Our house had become a temporary refuge for Sylvia's colleagues from around the Pacific. FSPI was holding its annual meeting in Suva, and for a week or so we found ourselves surrounded by people we had known since we first arrived in the South Pacific years ago. Work and family life blended easily on the islands, and it was heartening to watch the country director of FSP Kiribati give us news about our old dogs on Tarawa—still alive!—while Lukas dozed contentedly in her arms. Since our house was spilling over with people, and the little ratu's feet rarely touched the ground as he was passed around like a giggly talisman, I thought I'd spend a few days exploring some other corner of Fiji, and so I bought a ferry ticket to Savusavu on the island of Vanua Levu.

It occurred to me, as I made my arrangements for the fourteen-hour ferry voyage, that my aversion to flying on small aircraft had reached pathological proportions. Nevertheless, if there was a way to get to where I wanted to go without having to leave the Earth's surface, then I would choose that rather than fly. Even a raft would do.

"And how old is the boat?" I asked the ticket agent. I had seen some of the ferries that plied the waters of Fiji, shepherding people to the outer islands.

"Only nine years old," she said brightly.

As I soon discovered, she meant that it had been in Fiji for only nine years. *The Spirit of Fiji* was at least forty years old. "Be there at 10 A.M. sharp," the ticket agent had told me. The morning of our departure, I boarded the ship in industrial Walu Bay, and as I walked across the steel deck I noticed that the ship was deeply corroded. The paint peeled. Mechanics emerged from below deck carrying rusty machine parts, which they studied with considerable interest. Belching trucks rumbled aboard.

I handed my ticket to someone I presumed was a ship employee; no one was wearing a uniform. "First class," he said. He took a stamp, dipped it in ink, and stamped my forearm. FIRST CLASS, it said. This pleased me enormously. It was my first time traveling anywhere first class, and the stamp on my arm made it seem extra special. First class entitled me to a berth in a four-bunk cabin, an indulgence that cost $10 more than a standard fare. The lower classes, those not graced with stamps on their arms, were consigned to the deck. I found my cabin, deposited my backpack, and read the notice informing me that breakfast would be served between eight and nine, lunch from noon to one, tea from four to five, and dinner between seven and eight. *Very civilized*, I thought. As far as I could tell, I was the only passenger with a first-class stamp.

I spent a few minutes getting lost deep within the bowels of the boat. There were signs on the walls, but alas, they were in Greek. There was even a map of the Greek Isles. Eventually, I emerged on the upper deck and mingled among the commoners. Most of the passengers had settled on the benches and were busy eating their lunches. Soon the water below was marked with a confetti of plastic bags and wrappers.

We were due to leave imminently, and I found a perch from which to watch the event. Two hours later, I was still there, watching the mechanics hammer away at a greasy machine part. The boat hadn't moved. I should have known, of course. Even after nearly four years in the South Pacific, I still maintained an optimistic faith in schedules. But nothing leaves on time in the South Pacific, and when the *Spirit of Fiji* finally departed, three hours behind schedule, I realized that this would be a very long day, and suddenly I understood the appeal of flying.

The ship glided through the break in the reef, near a Chinese fishing boat that had missed the entrance and lay hull up on the reef shelf. Beyond the reef, there was a swell running, and the flat-bottomed ship rolled with each wave. We were traveling at approximately two miles per hour. I could swim faster, I thought. We passed the headlands of Viti Levu and threaded our way through the Lomaiviti archipelago toward Koro Island. In the distance, I could see the hazy contours of Wakaya Island, the destination of choice for movie stars and millionaires. The morning newspaper had informed us that Tom Cruise was presently frolicking on its beaches. I felt a camaraderie with Tom. We both traveled first class.

We moved over deep water, a wine-dark blue dappled by the sun. Behind us was the cragged eastern shore of Viti Levu. In the distance, the offshore islands reflected an alluring languor. A frigate bird swept low above the waves of the Koro Sea. If there was a more enchanting scene anywhere in the world, I could not imagine it. In gloomy Suva, with its fetid air and belching buses, paradise was a punch line. But here, on the glimmering water, I again understood the allure of Fiji. Paradise was a place that could be seen only from a distance, but it pleased me knowing that we lived so close to it.

The hours passed. Most of the other passengers had brought their own food and drink. I set off to see what I could find. Not quite thinking ahead, I had brought only a small bottle of water and a banana, which I had long ago finished. I checked the first-class lounge, prepared and even looking forward to waving my forearm about. I hadn't really expected an afternoon tea service. Indeed, what I had expected to find was the ship's crew snoring on the benches, which was precisely what I did find. Disappointed that no one had asked to see my stamp, I moved on to the general café. It was shuttered.

Now I was thirsty. I had had enough experience with waterborne intestinal parasites to make me wary of drinking the ship's water. The last thing I wanted to experience was belly-belly in Savusavu. This wasn't a Carnival cruise. This was a third-world interisland ferry. There wasn't a tourist aboard other than myself, and it seemed unlikely that the ship's water supply was any cleaner than that found flowing through the pipes in Suva. Still, I noticed that every half hour or so, a crewman carried a bucket of water up to the ship's bridge.

"They are drinking kava," a fellow passenger noted.

Oceans of it, apparently. As the sun set over the Koro Sea the kava was replenished bucket by bucket. If the crew was using the ship's water for kava, I figured, it might be drinkable. The captain, I noticed, hadn't withered away. Indeed, he was the most corpulent man I had ever seen in Fiji. He wore a red T-shirt, splotched with grease and oil, that strained to cover his enormous gut. A little belly-belly would probably do him some good. Nevertheless, though I was feeling parched, I resisted the temptation to drink the ship's water. I had just emerged from a bout of dengue fever—what fun that was—and was looking forward to a few weeks of health.

Shortly before midnight, we neared Koro Island. This should be interesting, I thought. There was no electricity on Koro. The only light available was offered by the stars. It was an extremely compact harbor, and the ship was very large. The captain and crew had spent the previous seven hours drinking buckets of kava. If it were me at the helm, I have no doubt we would have soon become one with the reef. In any event, the captain gave a few curt orders, and the ship turned around and brought its rump toward the pier in an admirable display of seamanship. They might not look like seamen, I thought. And they might all be stoned on kava. But they knew what they were doing. A few more trucks rumbled aboard, and soon we were cruising again through the darkness.

Two A.M. passed. Most of the passengers were asleep on the benches. Though I was exhausted, I couldn't sleep. I had tried to retire to my first-class bunk, but with every roll of the boat there followed a discordant creaking of metal grinding on metal. It was the kind of noise that I tend to fixate on, and after a half hour, I was reduced to a state of frothing insensibility. Resigned, I sat on the deck and watched the slow drift of stars moving over the sea. Seventeen hours on a ferry was beginning to feel very much like seventeen hours on a ferry. Indeed, I was beginning to check my watch an awful lot, wishing the time forward: 3:02 . . . 3:06 . . . 3:09. Finally, at 4 A.M.—there's that time again—we arrived at Savusavu, and the silence of the night was disturbed by the sound of a dozen trucks turning over their engines, sending forth a foul cloud of exhaust that hovered above us in the still air.

I grabbed my backpack and walked the short distance toward the town. It is often described as sleepy, and it was good and asleep now. I hadn't made any advance arrangement for a hotel, which now struck me as a regrettable oversight. Savusavu at 4 A.M. was a dim and quiet place where nothing stirred except for a few dogs. I picked up a rock and trudged on. I had almost resigned myself to simply holding out until dawn, when I came across a sign pointing me toward the Hot Springs Hotel. I followed the road up a hillside, pleased to see that, if all went well, I might soon be able to put an end to this day.

Suddenly, two dogs bounded out of the trees. *Well, fuck,* I thought, my heart pounding. Ever since we'd lived in Kiribati, I had become utterly terrified of island dogs. They are either wild animals, left to their own devices to find sustenance, or they have been trained as guard dogs. Neither type amused me. I stopped moving and dropped my backpack, poised to throw my rock. The dogs were about thirty feet away. They too stopped. I stomped my feet. "Skat! Get out of here!" I hissed. Off they ran. Apparently, they had learned to fear people. Thank goodness for that, I thought.

The hotel lobby was open to the elements. I was pleased to see a light on.

"Bula," said the sleepy guard, using the Fijian word for "hello."

"Bula," I said. "Do you have any water bottles here?"

They did not. A few moments later, I found myself in my hotel room, drinking from a flow of rusty tap water.

SAVUSAVU. It pleases me just to say the word. *Savusavu.* For a while, I had considered going to Taveuni, the garden isle of Fiji. There was a boat going there too. I had been to Taveuni before, when we traveled through Fiji on our return home from Kiribati to the U.S., and I had liked it very much. The main town on Taveuni is Somosomo. It was a close call, but Somosomo wasn't quite as evocative as Savusavu.

There was another reason for going to Savusavu. Many of the

Fijians on Vanua Levu had supported the coup, and I wanted to ask them, you know, what was up with that. It was difficult to get a sense of what had driven the coup in Suva. Fijians and Indians lived separate lives in the capital, but they lived these separate lives together, harmoniously ignoring each other, more or less. The Fijians played rugby, the Indians cricket. The Fijians worked in government. The Indians were the shopkeepers. The Fijians celebrated the queen's birthday. The Indians lit candles for Diwali, the Hindu festival of lights. Even though they had been sharing the islands for more than a hundred years in roughly equal numbers, intermarriage between Fijians and Indians was a striking rarity. In a way, Suva reminded me of Washington, where blacks and whites occupied the same geography, walked the same streets, shopped at the same stores, then went home to lives that had nothing to do with each other. In our Suva neighborhood, in the evenings, the Indians who lived below us gathered around a small set of drums and sang Hindu chants. The Fijians who lived above us settled around the kava bowl. And in the mornings, we all wished each other a good day.

Sylvia and I often went for early-morning walks along the seawall in Suva. It was the only place in town where one could have some confidence of walking without being assaulted by dogs. Some mornings we ran into Sitiveni Rabuka on his morning constitution, bedecked in a shimmering track suit. He had led Fiji for a decade following the first coup, after he overthrew the first predominantly Indian elected government. A little farther on, we often encountered Mahendra Chaudhry, the Indian prime minister of Fiji until George Speight and his followers attacked the parliament. That they could share the same seawall for their morning ambulation, I thought, was rather extraordinary and spoke well of Suva. Indeed, most Fijians in Suva voted for the Labor Party, Chaudhry's Indian-led party. On the western coast of Viti Levu, the sunny side, and up into the Mamanuca and Yasawa islands, there was little support for the coup among indigenous Fijians. So how could it happen? How could a democratically elected government be overthrown on an island where support for the coup was negligible?

It was a chiefly dispute, people said in Suva. In Fiji, a chief, or ratu, as we had learned, had considerable power. The vast majority of land in Fiji is Fijian owned, and rents, whether from an international resort or an Indian sugarcane farmer, are collected each month by the Native Lands Trust Commission and sent on to the local chiefs. These are inherited positions, and if there is a more lamentable form of governance than inherited power, I cannot imagine it. In Europe, of course, tax money is still dished out to a few royals. But today, this is really the equivalent of fattening up a duck for the hunt. In return for accepting the largesse of the people, the royals are subjected to hunters—known as paparazzi—who stalk them with zoom lenses, seeking out scintillating photos for the public. A good shot will result in abject humiliation and personal ruination for the royal, which strikes me as a fair bargain. Alas, Fijians still maintain a quaint reverence for all things chiefly, and when a paramount chief has dastardly deeds on his mind, there is little to stop him. It was the nefarious northern chiefs, people alleged, who were responsible for the coup and the subsequent army mutiny.

In Savusavu, however, I couldn't quite understand why anyone would bother to trouble himself with something as nettlesome as overthrowing a government. With the morning sun, Savusavu revealed itself to be located in one of the most extraordinarily beautiful settings I had ever encountered in the islands. The town overlooked Savusavu Bay, an alluring expanse of blue water hemmed in by verdant peaks. Directly across was a small islet, and in the safety between it and the main island, a number of yachts were riding out the hurricane season.

I ambled down toward the dozen or so clapboard buildings that constituted downtown Savusavu, and four minutes later, after I had wandered from one end of the muddy town to the other, I caught a taxi in front of the covered market. For such an extraordinary locale, Savusavu was a modest town.

"Where will you be going today, sir?"

Sir? I wasn't often called sir in Fiji. But then I noticed that I still had my FIRST CLASS stamp on my arm. I considered getting a tattoo to make it permanent.

I didn't really have a destination in mind, just a vague desire to see a bit of the island and perhaps have a swim somewhere. I told the driver as much.

"No problem, sir. I will show you the area around Savusavu, and then I will take you to the beach. You go for a swim, and I will come back for you after one hour. What do you think?"

This struck me as an excellent plan. The taxi driver's name was Saresh. He was an Indo-Fijian of a venerable age.

"I have one son who is a dentist in Canada," he said as we followed a paved road into the hills behind Savusavu. "Another son who is a welder in Christchurch, and a daughter who takes care of her children in Melbourne. She is married to an accountant. Then I have three more left here. A son who is an accountant in Suva, another who owns a garage here, and a daughter who is still a student. You see? Everybody working. Not like Fijian people."

It often struck me how Indians and Fijians viewed each other. Indians saw Fijians as a slothful and indulgent people who never thought of the future. Fijians saw Indians as busy worker bees who needed constant watching, lest they sneak off with Fijian land. In Suva, a multiracial city, such notions were softened through interaction. Elsewhere in Fiji, however, where Fijians and Indians did not live side by side, the prejudice festered.

"Look," Saresh said, waving at the thick bush that lined the road. "This is Fijian land. They don't do anything with it. No farms. Nothing. They lazy, you see. Now this," he said, gesturing toward a sculpted garden and a sumptuous house with views over Savusavu Bay, "is European land. Very tidy, you see."

There were a surprising number of Westerners in Savusavu, I learned, chasing paradise. They had built their bungalows on the ridges above the bay. Some of the homes were on freehold land, that small portion of island land that could be bought and sold. Other homes were on what was called native land, which could only be leased from the Fijian landowners.

"And see," Saresh continued, "this is an Indian village. It is free-hold land. You see? It is very clean. Everyone takes care of their house. Not like Fijian villages."

The village was in a deep gully below the road. It seemed like an awful location for a village, a place where breezes did not reach and mosquitoes festered. But it was freehold land, and that for the Indo-Fijians was what mattered most.

Saresh dropped me off at a small beach near the Namale Spa & Sanctuary. "It is very dear," he said as we passed the resort's entrance. That was Victorian English for "expensive." I had read that it was owned by Anthony Robbins, the toothy motivational speaker, and that it was frequently booked solid with convention-eers motivated to spend upwards of $2,000 a night. He's good, that Tony Robbins. My taxi fare, so far, had come to about $4, and as I swam I wondered if I would have enjoyed my swim more if I'd paid an additional $1,996. I'd probably enjoy it less, I thought, particu-larly as it was by then overcast. Foolishly, I failed to put on sun-screen, and when Saresh picked me up exactly one hour later, it was with some exasperation that I realized I was burned. Thank goodness, I thought, that at least I hadn't paid $2,000 for the privilege of getting a sunburn on an overcast day.

I asked Saresh what it had been like on Vanua Levu during the coup.

"During the coup, it was very bad. They attacked all the Indian houses here. They take the cattle and the goats and the chickens. They take the women. They even took the Air Fiji pilots hostage. It was not so bad in Savusavu, but here," he said, gesturing toward the hills and the Indian farms, "it was very bad. And in Lambasa, it was also very bad."

Lambasa was a town in the north of Vanua Levu. It was largely an Indian town, and since the coup, many of its inhabitants had drifted to Suva looking for work. This had been a region for growing sugarcane, a precarious industry in the best of times. Since the coup, however, many Fijian landowners had declined to renew the leases of Indo-Fijian sugarcane farmers. Expelled from the land their families had farmed for generations, the farmers found themselves in an unenviable situation.

"For me it is too late," Saresh said. "I will die in Fiji. But for my children, I tell them to study. They must study, get degrees, and then they can emigrate."

Why couldn't we all just get along? I thought. Perhaps we could just blame the British for Fiji's predicament. After all, it was they who had brought the Indians—coolies is what they called them—to Fiji. The British had needed Fiji to pay for itself, and rather than disrupt traditional Fijian society, they had decided to import workers from abroad to till the soil. Fijian and Indian cultures are disparate, to say the least. And yet, Fiji had been an independent country for more than thirty years. That these two peoples could not reconcile themselves to each other was a failure of their leaders.

A SHORT WHILE LATER, I found myself at the Captain's Café in Savusavu, admiring a framed note hanging on the wall. It was from Brooke Shields, who had apparently enjoyed her meal there. Some of Fiji's higher-end resorts were on Vanua Levu. Would Brooke Shields stay in a resort? I wondered. No, I figured. She probably visited Savusavu on a yacht. Such were the depths of my thoughts when a Fijian man joined me at my table overlooking the harbor.

"Bula," he said. "I am Bill."

He wore a formal sulu, the sort typically worn by Fijian men on their way to the Methodist church on Sundays.

"These are the end days," he informed me.

"Ah . . . ," I said. "Could be, could be." I didn't have any information suggesting otherwise, so I thought it best to remain neutral.

"I was hit on the head," he said, rubbing the back of his head.

"I see."

"By a truck."

"Ah . . ."

"I was in the army. But I didn't receive anything. No money. Nothing."

Clearly, Bill was not one for small talk. I wasn't quite sure what to say to him, and so I spent a moment nodding thoughtfully, a little nonverbal gesture that I hoped conveyed a sense that I too found this world lamentable.

"So, Bill," I said. "Savusavu is in the province of Cakaudrove?"

"Yes, Cakaudrove. Then there is Bua and Taveuni. Taveuni is where the high chief is from."

All coup support areas.

"So you have a chiefly system here," I said. I found it helpful to feign ignorance, though often enough, it wasn't much of a feint. The Fijian chiefly system was exasperatingly complex. Even the president of the Great Council of Chiefs, the chief chief, if you will, had recently had to plead his case to a special tribunal of chiefs when he attempted to claim a particular title. A chiefly cousin had also claimed the title. It took months of painstaking research into their respective lineages before the tribunal decided in the chief chief's favor. This was no small matter, however. An air of latent violence had hung in the air in Fiji as the chiefs sorted through the dispute.

Of course, I wasn't the only foreigner who had trouble understanding chiefly ways in Fiji. Sylvia's boss, Rex, had once recounted the story of a freshly arrived diplomat from England.

"She had arrived at a kava ceremony for a chief taking a new title, a very important ceremony," Rex told us. "Well, this English diplomat is talking and talking to the other diplomats, and she sees this *bure*—a ceremonial meeting hall—with sides that hang nearly to the ground. She sees all these shoes on the outside, so she takes her shoes off, and as she steps inside she sees in front of the chief a big bowl of what looks like muddy water."

"Oh, no."

"Yes. The kava. She walks up to it, dips her feet into it, and begins to wash her feet in the kava. A week later, she was reassigned to another country."

Fijians, as I had already learned, do not have a sense of humor when it comes to their chiefs.

"Yes, we have chiefs here," Bill continued. "Ratus."

"What if you have a bad chief?" I asked. "Can the people do anything about it?"

"It is not the Fijian way."

Which, in my humble opinion, is a problem. George Speight had been a mere front man, the public face of the coup. No commoner in Fiji could topple a democratically elected government without the consent of a few powerful chiefs.

"The problem," Bill said, looking me in the eye, "is Western influence."

Oh, well then. Bill was frisky. And which Western influences would those be? Democracy? As a Westerner, I will take the blame for global warming, third-world debt, rising sea levels, war—the big ones, in any case—and Britney Spears. But I don't think that's what Bill had in mind. It raised my hackles. But then I thought about it for a moment, and I had to concede that to a certain degree he was right. The chiefly system that exists today is in fact a legacy of colonial English rule. It was the colonists who created the Great Council of Chiefs to further English power. Today, it is often referred to as the Great Council of Thieves. The chiefly system in Fiji was, at worst, a rapacious kleptocracy and, at best, a stubborn, ill-serving adherence to a colonial era that has long since vanished.

And yet, though colonialism and modernity had changed Fiji, the chiefs still fought the battles of yore. There are three traditional chiefly confederations in Fiji, and the coup can best be understood as a battle among the confederations for preeminence. Racial tensions were not so much a cause of the coup as a weapon the chiefs could use to further their ends. George Speight found himself isolated on Nukulau Island not because he overthrew an Indian-led government but because his actions had forced the resignation of Fiji's president, Ratu Mara, a preeminent chief. Speight would not have survived a day if he had been placed inside the Suva Prison. The Fijian prisoners who were loyal to Ratu Mara would have killed him in an instant.

I asked Bill what it had been like on Vanua Levu during the coup.

"No problem," he said. "It was very quiet."

SAVUSAVU WAS A PLACE to disappear. It was far away. It was un-
crowded. It was lush and beautiful. It even smelled nice, with the
scent of bougainvillea and hibiscus wafting through the sea air. The
town itself wasn't much to look at. It was merely a length of simple
shops that catered to the needs of its inhabitants. But the setting was
extraordinary, and it attracted escapists from around the world.

The following evening, after I had spent the afternoon cautiously paddling a rented kayak around Savusavu Bay, I stopped by
the Planter's Club. I had been told that this was where the mixed-
race people drank. Outside of Suva, I was learning, Fiji was a remarkably race-obsessed country. There were indigenous Fijians and
Indo-Fijians, of course, and there were kaivalangis like myself, and
there were a good number of Fijians with a dollop of Gilbertese or
Tongan or Scottish blood coursing through their veins, enough to
ensure that they too were barred from owning land. The shape of
your nose and the amount of melatonin in your skin determined
the course of your life in Fiji.

"This is for members only," said the security guard outside the
appealing wooden archway.

"Oh," I said. "Well, do you think I can go in anyway?"

"Yes, no problem."

Inside, I felt as if I had stepped into a honky-tonk tavern somewhere in Kentucky. There was even country music. I had never before been much of a fan of country music, but after my ears had
been subject to months of nothing but the harsh warble of Indian
pop music, I was ready to line dance with a possum. In a corner, a
group of men played darts and drank beer. I sidled up to the bar,
next to a couple speaking German. I drank a beer with the hopeful

expectation that someone would talk to me, but after one Fiji Bitter passed and I was well on my way through another without anyone's acknowledging my existence, I went ahead and barged into my neighbor's conversation.

"Du bist Deutsche?" I said, asking the obvious. When I have to speak German, I simply speak Dutch with a German accent in the hope that my listener will soon catch on that I don't really speak German, and then we'll both happily move on to English.

"Fiji is shit," the woman said after we'd established that her English was better than my German. "A big shit."

This seemed a little negative to me. I could understand a disparaging comment or two directed toward Suva. But—provided, of course, that one ignored the politics on Vanua Levu, and the recent strife, and the despondent Indians, and the corrupt chiefs—well, Savusavu seemed pretty *wunderbar* to me.

"Eight years I have lived here. And I have had enough. Enough! I am going back to Germany. Savusavu is a shit. Fiji is a shit."

"What's wrong with Savusavu?" I asked.

"Everything. The electricity doesn't work. The telephones don't work. And if you don't have freehold land, then everything is a big shit. I want to build another house. I fill out papers and nothing happens. I fill out more papers and nothing happens. I drink kava with the fucking chief and finally, okay, I can build. And so I hire the Fijians to clear the bush. I give them money. And nothing happens. So I drink more kava with the fucking chief. He says okay, he'll send the men. And then nothing. Fiji is a big shit. I have had enough."

And with that she stormed out without so much as an *auf Wiedersehen*, her mute companion trailing after her. I felt for her. It was a lamentation often expressed by those from northern climes who had moved to the islands expecting palm trees and beaches and strumming ukuleles. All that exists, of course, but it doesn't take long to become jaded by one's surroundings, and what remains, then, is nothing more than day-to-day life. She had moved to Savusavu, I suspected, because it offered paradise at a good price. But what she had regarded as paradise—the unspoiled land, the pace of life, the depth of the island culture—was what made day-to-day life so exasperating for her. Plus, she was German.

I moved on to Savusavu's other drinking establishment. There were only two: the Planter's Club and the Copra Shed Marina, which was the preserve of the yachties. These were no dilettantes, fluttering their sails on weekends as they stood at the wheel with a rakish captain's cap on their head and a gin and tonic in their hand. In fact, a surprising number of the yachties here were families who had anchored their boats in the safe confines of Savusavu harbor to ride out the cyclone season. In the mornings, they home-schooled, or boat-schooled, their kids. In the afternoon, the children, who ranged from the ages of about five up to thirteen, were free to race one another up and down the harbor in dinghies. This was deeply unfair, I thought, recalling that when I was a youngster in Canada, I'd had to get up well before dawn to deliver newspapers by sled through the cold, cold darkness.

The bar looked out over the harbor, and as I watched the yachtie kids playing with the Fijian kids—a little tableau of multiracial harmony—I was suddenly seized with a deep pang of longing for my little one. How excellent it must be, sailing across the expanse of the Pacific with your family, spending a few months or a few years on an island and moving on as whim determined. "Not with this wife," Sylvia had said when I'd expressed my longing for a life at sea back in Port Vila. A fantasy, then, it would likely remain.

"Hey, man," said one of the patrons. "You're Steve, right? You play the trombone."

"No, sorry, you must have me confused with someone else."

"You're not Steve?" he said, giving me a bleary-eyed look. "Well, who are you, man?"

It was like meeting the Dennis Hopper character in *Apocalypse Now*. He called himself John.

"It's about the solitude, man," he replied when I asked him about his boat. "If you can deal with solitude, you can deal with anything. You don't need no $200-an-hour psychoanalyst, man. Just sail a boat for forty days and forty nights and you deal with all kinds of shit. HA HA HA."

It had been a long, strange trip for John.

"Yeah, I was in Vietnam, man. How could you tell? HA HA HA. It's 'cause we're all fucked up, right? I did underwater demolitions, but I didn't kill anybody. I don't want to talk about that, man. HA HA."

John had been sailing for eight years. I couldn't imagine how he'd endured it. He was a bundle of loose nerves, trembling in a way that suggested a man off his meds. Most of the yachties I had met were calm and cerebral, the kind of people who happily spend an entire day methodically sanding an oar so that it moves through the water with perfect efficiency. John just twitched. He was a lone sailor. It had taken him forty days to sail from Panama to the Marquesas.

"Solitude, man. It makes you stronger. I spent three years in Alaska, man. I lived in the fucking woods. Only went into town once a month. HA HA."

I asked him where he'd been in the Pacific.

"Everywhere, man. Tahiti, Tonga, New Zealand, the Cooks. They charge $15 a day to dock in the Cooks, man. I was out of there in nine days."

I wondered how he lived. "Do you do charters?" I asked. For cash, many of the yachties chartered their boats.

"Charters," John sputtered. "Oh, no. Then you got to take care of them, give them drinks, have a license. HA HA. No."

The sun had set, leaving a blue twilight.

"I got married, man," John said. "Fijian woman. Having a baby. HA HA."

"So are you settling in Savusavu?" I asked.

"I don't know. Yeah, sure. Who fucking cares? You might say I've dropped out of society."

I had a sense that John would keep moving, that he would keep looking for something, unsure of what precisely he was looking for. I understood the feeling. It wasn't long ago that I too had felt the twitching restlessness. Paradise was always over there, a day's sail away. But it's a funny thing, escapism. You can go far and wide and you can keep moving on and on through places and years, but somehow you never escape your own life. I, finally, knew where my life belonged. Home.

CHAPTER 14

In which the author and his wife decide to depart the islands of the South Pacific and return to the United States, which strikes most people—even most Americans they know—as utterly insane, all things considered, but they do it anyway, because now, at last, for the first time ever, they find themselves yearning for home.

IT'S FUNNY HOW TIME PASSES WHEN YOU HAVE A CHILD. Before Lukas arrived, I had always been able to press the pause button on life. I'd find a nice place somewhere between jobs and rest there for a while, a still life in a moving picture. But there was no pausing with Lukas. Just as I'd grown accustomed to his ability to sit upright on his own, he went ahead and started crawling. Once Lukas was mobile, life became a chase, and just as we thought we had caught up to him, we'd find him standing, tentatively perched on wobbly legs, holding on to a chair, first with two hands and then one, contemplating whether to let go and take those first steps. No, there was no pausing now.

Sylvia and I had decided it was time to stop looking for paradise. It would always be just out of reach, a shimmering mirage on the horizon. There was only one place where one might find paradise: home. We didn't quite know where home was, but we thought we'd look for it in America.

"Are we crazy?" Sylvia asked.

"Very possibly," I said.

Our friends in the U.S. certainly thought so. America had embarked on an endless war, and the world had begun to turn its back on it. The U.S. was a different place now, we were told. Well, we thought. So was Fiji. The villages were being emptied of men, lured by the dollars to be found working for U.S. military contractors in Kuwait and Iraq. More than a few had already returned to Fiji in body bags. It struck me as just a trifle presumptuous to start a war and then hire villagers from Fiji to fight it. Escapism, clearly, was futile. Who could know where the world was headed? The best we could do, we figured, was to ensure that Lukas had as many nationalities as he could, so that, no matter what, he'd always have a place to go. Within his first year alone, he had acquired Dutch, Canadian, and American passports. Should events warrant, he could pick up a Fijian one too. It made us feel like good parents, knowing that if the world went to hell, he'd have options.

In the meantime, however, we thought it might be nice to raise him in the same hemisphere as the rest of his family. Clearly, our priorities had changed. Distressed to see pictures of her grandson wearing nothing more than a diaper and a tank top, my mother had begun to send packages of fluffy baby garb from Ralph Lauren. Someone in her family was going to wear Polo, and Lukas was her last hope. It seemed cruel to deny her, and moving to a climate where we could fulfill my mother's sartorial preferences seemed like the right thing to do. Sylvia and I were hardwired for change, for hopping on airplanes every two years and beginning anew. But this was going to be a different kind of change, and this time it would take us away from Oceania.

In Fiji, as in Vanuatu, we were expatriates. This is different from being a mere foreigner. When we'd lived in Kiribati, the islanders regarded us as curiosities—a little peculiar, perhaps, often in need of guidance, and certainly *foreign*. But it wasn't long before we were seen as locals. We ate the same fish, sang the same songs—or at least the one song we knew the words to—and exchanged the same parasites. We experienced the island much as the I-Kiribati did. Partly, of course, this was because there was no other way to experience it. The isolation was absolute, the deprivation universal. Living on an atoll was like living on a boat. It didn't matter if you were rich or poor, native or foreign. You rolled with the same waves.

The expatriate life was different, however. It could certainly be seductive. Our dollars went far in Fiji, and on many weekends we still found ourselves at lushly landscaped island resorts, where we'd linger in the warm shallows of the South Pacific as Lukas splashed gleefully about. We could afford a car, a nice house with a view, though not, apparently, a backyard, and when we needed to see a doctor, we went to the same doctors who attended to the ratus. But living as an expatriate can warp you. Every Friday, I picked up a week's worth of *International Herald Tribune*s from Bill, an American expatriate who had lived in Fiji for twenty years. He was an accountant for an international aid organization, and while there was no shortage of accountants in Fiji, he had managed to linger on with an expat's tax-free salary and benefits. Most afternoons, he could be found on the golf course, his membership charged to a child-nutrition program. The *IHT*, which was obscenely expensive in Fiji, was paid for by a disaster-training project. While we didn't think it likely that we'd ever end up as ethically challenged as Bill—though who can say for sure?—we nevertheless regarded him as a cautionary tale about the perils of the expatriate life. His kids were lost souls, born on the islands but not of the islands. As the children of expatriates, they didn't fit into the complex social milieu of Fiji. Nor, having grown up on the islands, did they move comfortably in America. The oldest had returned to Fiji after attending a community college in Hawaii for three months. It was "too stressful," he said. The only reason Bill subscribed to the *International Herald Tribune* was so that he could check the box scores for his favorite baseball team, the Cleveland Indians, which I found a little sad.

We didn't want Lukas to be unduly stressed should fate lead him toward a community college in Hawaii. Indeed, if he didn't realize that he was very, very lucky to have parents who would send him to community college in Hawaii, then we would have failed in our parental obligations. Our first priority, clearly, was to provide him with a home, and while most of our friends couldn't quite comprehend our decision to leave Fiji for a country that had evidently lost its mind, geopolitically speaking, the parents among them did.

As we began packing we discovered that we now had *stuff*. There was a crib, a changing table, and a rocking chair, the beginnings of a household. The rest of our belongings were scooped up by friends in Suva. After much discussion, we decided that we would return to Washington, where we had a concentration of friends and family. It would be different this time, we thought. We weren't so foolish, however, as to make such a move without first stopping over in Hawaii, where we hoped to ease our transition back to the United States, and possibly check out the community colleges, just in case.

Before we left, Anna invited us to her village for a traditional *lovo*, a feast cooked in a freshly dug earth oven. Though close to Suva, the village of Wailoko was another world. Inside this hamlet, surrounded by steep, verdant hills, the bustle of Suva seemed distant. Upon our arrival, we were garlanded with flowers. Even Lukas found himself bedecked in a floral necklace. Soon he was being passed from villager to villager, hailed as Ratu Lukas.

"I wonder if he'll get this kind of attention in the U.S.," Sylvia mused. "Look, even the ten-year-old boys want to play with him."

Inside the pit, Anna's sons had lit a fire, and as the wood burned they added stones to the blaze. A pig had been slaughtered, and when the stones were sufficiently hot, the pork, as well as taro and pumpkin, were wrapped in banana leaves and placed on the rocks. Then dirt was shoveled onto the meal, and as dinner cooked we sat on mats inside Anna's modest two-room home. On her walls, there were pictures, many of them faded, of all the children she had helped raise over the years.

"You know that money you gave me for Christmas?" Anna said. "I used it to start a business."

"Really," I said, feeling very pleased.

"Yes. I bought a sty, and now I make the grog and sell it."

Anna had entered the moonshine business. We were so proud.

Her extended family was gathered around the kava bowl. I didn't know when next I'd find myself sitting around a kava bowl, so I savored every bitter shell.

"You don't have kava in America?" asked Peter, Anna's oldest son.

"Sadly, no."

"But I thought you could find everything in America."

"Not kava, alas."

We pondered this tragic state of affairs for a moment. I hadn't left the Pacific yet and already I was beginning to miss it enormously. To spend a few hours clustered around a kava bowl, even one containing Fijian kava, in the company of friends and family had come to exemplify the civilized life for me. Lukas too apparently agreed. He had spent the afternoon in the arms of the village, and now as he descended back to earth, he launched himself like a rocket in diapers, crawling straight for the kava bowl.

Anna laughed. "Just like his father."

"The apple doesn't fall far from the tree," Sylvia added.

Good boy, I thought. Always be true to your roots.

AUTHOR'S NOTE

Among the books I consulted in researching the region, several proved particularly useful. *To Kill a Bird with Two Stones* by Jeremy MacClancy is, to the best of my knowledge, the only general history book on Vanuatu. Ron Crocombe's *The South Pacific* provides an excellent survey of the region. *Fiji's Times: A History of Fiji* by Kim Gravelle offers a very lively account of that country's past. Though first published in 1858, *Fiji and the Fijians: The Islands and Their Inhabitants* by the Reverend Thomas Williams remains among the most insightful books delving into traditional Fiji.

ACKNOWLEDGMENTS

Every writer likes a challenge. Actually, that's probably not true. Nevertheless, as I began to think about this book, this second book, I wondered, what could I do to make the process of writing it a little more challenging. I thought long and hard about it, and decided that on a scale of difficulty, having a baby—a second child—three months before a deadline would rank pretty high. And so this is what I did. Not entirely by myself, of course. But I was there. As I cradled the littlest one with one hand while assembling a Hot Wheels Super 6 in 1 Motorized Race Track with the other—a toy loved equally by father and firstborn son—my wife made the utterly baseless observation that I might be procrastinating. I wasn't procrastinating at all, however. I was *parenting*. Still, when my deadline began to recede into the dim mists of time, and I turned my attention to Chapter 3, I thought, what else could I do to make the writing of this book a little more arduous? I pondered this for a long while and decided that this would be an excellent time to sell our house. So that is what we did.

As you may have surmised, I belong to the how-not-to-write-a-book school of writing. Fortunately, I am also very lucky. Ann Campbell, my editor at Broadway Books, remained unflappable and gracious as she sharpened and prodded the book to life under incredible time pressures. Among the good folks at Broadway, I'd also like to acknowledge Ursula Cary, Joanna Pinsker, and the mysterious "production people": Rebecca Holland, Nora Reichard, and Barbara Barthelmes. Apparently, I made their work . . . er, challenging. BJ Robbins, my supercool agent, injected humor and levity into my world whenever I needed it. In the Pacific, of the many, many islanders I am grateful to, I want to particularly acknowledge Rex Horoi and the people at FSP. Above all, I am profoundly grateful to my wife, Sylvia, whom, as they say, I owe big time.

J. Maarten Troost is the bestselling author of *The Sex Lives of Cannibals: Adrift in the Equatorial Pacific*. His essays have appeared in the *Atlantic Monthly,* the *Washington Post,* and the *Prague Post*. He lives with his wife and two sons in California.